Torah To Calvary
Series: Book I

Follow the Sign

TORAH TO CALVARY SERIES: BOOK I

Follow the Sign

By Gralin W. Buratt

LAURUS BOOKS

All scripture quotations, unless otherwise indicated, are taken from the HOLY BIBLE, NEW INTERNATIONAL VERSION®, NIV®. Copyright © 1973, 1978, 1984 by International Bible Society. Used by permission of Zondervan. All rights reserved.

Scripture quotations marked NKJV are taken from the New King James Version. Copyright © 1982 by Thomas Nelson, Inc. Used by permission. All rights reserved.

Scripture quotations marked KJV are from the King James Version of the Bible.

TORAH TO CALVARY SERIES: BOOK I

Follow the Sign
By Gralin W. Buratt

Copyright © 2020 by Gralin W. Buratt

All rights reserved. This book is protected under the copyright laws of the United States of America. This book may not be copied or reprinted for commercial gain or profit. The use of short quotations or occasional page copying for personal or group study is permitted and encouraged. Permission will be granted on request.

Paperback: ISBN: 978-1-943523-81-8

Mobi (Kindle): ISBN: 978-1-943523-82-5

ePub (iBooks, Nook): ISBN: 978-1-943523-83-2

Published by LAURUS BOOKS

LAURUS BOOKS
THE LAURUS COMPANY, INC.
www.TheLaurusCompany.com

This book may be purchased in paperback from TheLaurusCompany.com, Amazon.com, and most other retailers around the world. Available to retailers in Spring Arbor. May also be available in formats for electronic readers from their respective stores.

Dedication

Dedicated to
Christians and Jews
who worship in the
Name of Yeshua HaMashiach,
Jesus Christ.

Acknowledgments

A book with all of this information could never
have been written without the aid of many people.

It would be impossible to list all of them here, but I am
especially indebted to the following people and research books.

My thanks to Dr. Thomas W. Butler for his encouragement
in continuing to write this book, which was invaluable.

"Thank you" to Linda Millet who gave herself to helping this work
become reality. Her many hours of work are deeply appreciated.

Complete Jewish Bible, King James Version Bible

Likrat Shabbat - **Rabbi Sidney Greenburg**

Foxe's Book of Martyrs - **John Foxe**

**Earliest Christian Church found in Israeli jail -
Tim Butcher in Jerusalem**

Preface

This work, Book 1 of the Torah To Calvary Series, is a work of fiction based upon true biblical stories. It takes us into the private daily lives of a few of those in the early church at Antioch and some of those whom they influenced. The Hebrew language gives us insight into this early church, its history, and how they came to be called "Christians." It gives us a glimpse into how they grew in spiritual maturity and the influence of Jewish worship. Research for this book came from extensive biblical studies and travels to both Israel and Greece.

I grew up in South Louisiana, USA, where I attended church at an early age with my grandmother and received the gift of salvation at the age of ten. I was living in an abusive situation at home and always found refuge by reading the Bible.

One day, I was reading Deuteronomy 6:4-9. I read that I was to tie the Scriptures to my arm and wear them on my forehead as reminders. After reading this, I went to the barn and took straps and wound them around my arm and brought them to my forehead. I made a small leather box, wrote the 23rd Psalm on a piece of paper, and put it in the box around my forehead.

Many years later, God revealed to me what I had done. There was no one around me who could tell me what I had made or the meaning of it because it was a Jewish practice, and they were not Jews.

I later graduated from Kingsway Missionary Institute in McAllen, Texas. I did missionary work in the City of Victoria, Mexico, and pastored in the State of Tennessee for many years.

Eventually, I moved to Las Vegas, Nevada, to work and send my children through college. There, I started to find some Jewish roots and began to do some serious research on my family history. I made a trip to Israel, Greece, and the Greek Islands.

When I was at the Wailing Wall in Jerusalem, I understood the full meaning of what had happened to me as a child. For years, I had spoken to ministers about the leather straps and the strange things I was led to do with them. No one seemed to understand. I know now it was because they were not Jewish and did not understand Jewish practices. By that point, I knew that Jewish roots had been found in my family ancestry.

On my first trip to Israel, I did the purification ritual of cleansing the hands at the Wailing Wall and entered in on the Jewish side. While starting to pray, I was approached by six Jews bound with leather straps on their arms and head and the small leather box on their foreheads. I was paralyzed and fell to the ground. I cried to ELOHIM (God the Creator) with all of my heart. I had finally found my existence. I knew that I had made the Jewish *tefillin* without any knowledge of what I was doing. A blood test was done and confirmed what I knew in my heart, that I was Jewish by blood.

In Las Vegas, shortly after that, I began a study of Hebrew with the wife of a rabbi. I started going to a Jewish Synagogue to develop an ear for learning the language. It was very strange at first but became easier as time passed and we moved through the festival holidays. I also began to work with the Messianic Jews.

I have dedicated my life to teaching Torah to Calvary. I attend all Christian churches with my *tallit* (Jewish prayer shawl) and *yamaka* (Jewish skull cap). The Lord has opened doors in all denominations for me to speak of the link between the Old Testament Covenant and the New Testament Covenant of Yeshua HaMashaiach, Jesus the Messiah—the Torah became flesh and dwelt among us. I promote this message to the Jews.

This book will be translated into many languages, and the proceeds will be used to feed widows and orphans in many countries around the world. We hope you enjoy Book I in the "Torah to Calvary" Series, **Follow the Sign**. Be sure to watch for Book II coming soon. ➤

Table of Contents

Dedication..5
Acknowledgments..6
Preface..7
Prologue..11
Chapter 1..13
Chapter 2..17
Chapter 3..21
Chapter 4..25
Chapter 5..29
Chapter 6..33
Chapter 7..37
Chapter 8..41
Chapter 9..45
Chapter 10..47
Chapter 11..51
Chapter 12..53
Chapter 13..57
Chapter 14..59
Chapter 15..61
Chapter 16..63
Chapter 17..65
Chapter 18..67
Chapter 19..69
Chapter 20..71
Chapter 21..73
Chapter 22..75
Chapter 23..77
Chapter 24..79
Chapter 25..83
Chapter 26..85

Chapter 27	87
Chapter 28	89
Chapter 29	91
Chapter 30	93
Chapter 31	95
Chapter 32	97
Chapter 33	99
Chapter 34	101
Chapter 35	103
Chapter 36	105
Epilogue	107
Cast of Characters	109
Glossary	111
Photos from Israel, the Mediterranean, and the Middle East	113

Prologue

"This is Howard Beck reporting for the National Evening News. It is November 6, 2005. At the top of the news tonight, we find an interesting story in Megiddo Prison in Israel. An Israeli prisoner was removing rubble from the site of a new prison ward where he uncovered the edge of a large mosaic. It is said to be the site of the Holy Land's oldest church by a team of archaeologists.

"The discovery of the church at Megiddo is near the biblical site of Armageddon. It was hailed by experts as an important discovery that could reveal details of early Christians in the region. The church dated from the third century, around the time Constantine legalized Christianity across the Byzantine Empire.

"Head archaeologist, Yoton Tepper, said it is the oldest site of church remains ever found in Israel and maybe in the entire region. There has been much excitement about the discovery, with Prime Minister Oriel Sharon calling the discovery of the church 'an amazing story'! Inmates worked for months to uncover all of the mosaic, using sponges and buckets of water.

Inmates found two mosaics inside the church embedded in the foundation. One of the mosaics was covered with colorful fish. The other mosaic was an ancient Christian symbol that predated the widespread use of the cross. It told the story of a Roman officer and a woman named Aketous who donated money to build the church in memory of the One True God, 'Yeshua'.

"What significance do the mosaic tile and the sign of the fish have in Christian history?"

As the reporter moved on with the remaining news, theologians and Bible scholars around the world were left to ponder the question. What was the entire story? ➤

Follow the Sign

Chapter 1

It seemed like time had hidden itself as Ignatius gazed upon the waters of the Orontes River. So much had transpired in the last four days that he could not keep his thoughts in order. If only he had been at home in Antioch three days prior, maybe things would have been different.

Ignatius was pastor at the church in Antioch. He had traveled forty-three miles south to Laodicea to hear a prophet who been scheduled to speak in the house of Pamphilus of Caesarea. A meeting of this type was considered unlawful and could bring persecution to all present. There were always fabricated tales composed in order to injure the Christians and Jews. If they were brought before the magistrates, a test of oath was proposed. If they refused to take it, death was pronounced against them. Such was the infatuation of the pagans, that if famine, pestilence, or earthquakes afflicted any of the Roman provinces, the blame lay heavily upon the Christians and the Jews.

Ignatius could not hold back the tears. The deep heaviness of sorrow and grief weighed tightly on his chest. He stood paralyzed with fear, not knowing what to do. Is there anyone left alive from the church at Antioch? His own mother and father had been among the massive slaughter of eight hundred Christians. The news had reached him about mid-morning, halfway from Laodicea.

How could the government take such a stand against the poor and innocent? The political arena was responsible for drawing the swords. Those in high places knew how to inflict pain. However, their lives would be changed forever. Ignatius looked up into the sky and whispered, "Adonai, Heaven is more than our destination. It is our destiny."

The church had needed a bishop four years prior. Peter, the disciple of Yeshua, established the work many years earlier. Some say that while being sent from Syria to Rome, he was given up to the wild beasts to be devoured. It is also said of him that when he passed through Asia, being under the strict custody of his keeper, he strengthened and confirmed the churches throughout all the cities as he went with both exhortations and preaching of the Word of God.

His words were clearly remembered, saying, "Now I begin to be a disciple. I care for nothing of visible or invisible things, so that I may but win Christ. Let fire and the cross, let the breaking of bones and tearing of limbs, let the grinding of the whole body and all the malice of the devil come upon me, be it so, only may I win Christ Jesus." It was a privilege to succeed him as bishop of the church after his premature death.

Ignatius' father and mother embraced the new religion many years ago. He was raised to fear God. He received God's spirit into his life at the age of ten. His education consisted of a study of the Patriarchs, the Torah, Isaiah, Psalms, Proverbs, the Major Prophets, and the Minor Prophets. On his sixteenth birthday, his father gave him a copied manuscript of the apostles' teachings. Since his father was a carpenter, he was a skilled artisan of wood. Ignatius specialized in carving doors and making furniture. He always knew that the Lord had a plan for his life. God's will was the most important thing to find. His father taught him that following the will of God brings much persecution and many trials. The Word teaches that the believers are subject to suffering with Him if they are going to reign with Him.

Now, Ignatius was waiting at the banks of the river with his wife and three children. Titus his nephew was visiting for the summer and traveling with them. The city lay beyond the steep rocky hills about six furlongs east of the Kings Highway. His deepest desire was to console the believers in their hour of distress. However, how could he put his family in such danger?

Tired, exhausted, and overwhelmed by pain and grief, Ignatius began to pray: "Oh, my Lord, God of Abraham, Isaac, and Jacob, God that has come to us in the flesh, I worship You. The fear that I have feared has come upon us. How can men have so much hatred in their hearts to do such evil deeds? Lord, we need your comfort and security. I know not what awaits me in the city. I need your direction because I am helpless. I wait upon Thee. Hear my prayers, O Mighty God. Direct my path; send Your Holy Spirit to guide me. This I pray in the name of Yeshua."

Lydia could see how weak her husband was. He was never to show his fears. She knew this from the time they met nine years ago. Lydia was given to the Lord's service at an early age. She had been raised on a farm near the outskirts of the City of Antioch.

Lydia's father owned one of the largest olive orchards in the country. He had a basalt olive press capable of producing thousands of barrels of olive oil for export. Her family was Jewish by birth. They converted to Christianity many years ago. Her family was dedicated to the house of the Lord and to prayer. They helped spread the Word of the Lord throughout Antioch. It was at a cottage meeting that she first saw Ignatius. She was drawn to him by his handsome face and muscular frame. There was something in his voice that could calm troubled waters, a tenderness that touched her very soul.

It was hard to feed the children knowing that Ignatius had been fasting for three days. The believers at Laodicea had supplied them with bread, wine, and fresh fruit for their journey home. The small tent that they erected was a gift from Ignatius' father, given to him from the Apostle Paul. It gave them small comfort from the scorching sun.

Titus enjoyed visiting the family each summer. He felt something unique about Ignatius, his uncle, who had taught him the plan of salvation at an early age. It was last summer that he was baptized with believers at the river, submerged in water. The Spirit of the Lord engulfed his body and took control, for he spoke in tongues as the Spirit gave utterance. Titus dedicated his life to the work of the Lord. The past year, he had struggled with the decision of what to do with his life. He was seventeen years old with no definite plans. Maybe this summer that would change for him.

The family slept silently as Ignatius rose early to know what to do. God was their Protector and Provider. He would not leave them helpless. After much travailing in prayer, the Holy Spirit caused a deep sleep to fall upon him. He heard a voice say, "Fear not, for I am with thee. My angels shall guard the camp and protect thee from the enemy. In two days, load up thy belongings and travel southeast to Seleucia for a day's journey. There my servant awaits you. Listen to his words he will speak to you. Fear not, for I am with you. Look for the sign of the fish."

After much prayer, Ignatius meditated on the Lord and thought about all of the events that led to the destruction of the church in Antioch.

Follow the Sign

Chapter 2

The afternoon sun was beaming down on the dome of the temple of Isis. It was located on the highest hill in the city. Aketous was waiting for the sun to set before entering the carved wooden doors.

Instructions had been given by the high priest to be there on the night of the full moon.

For six years, she had tried to conceive. Her only possible happiness in life was to give birth to a child. Her husband, Antibus, refused to believe she was barren. She had long, wavy blonde hair, with eyes as blue as the Mediterranean Sea. Her skin was a dark olive color and velvety soft to the touch. Antibus spoke to the high priest and paid two thousand drachmas to set up the appointment. She would spend the night in the temple. The fertility god would find favor in her.

The temple was elaborately decorated with three shrines housed in a wall niche. Dark silk curtains of various colors covered the dingy gray walls. There were three altars parallel to the bronze statue of Isis. Only one had a flame. She could see the fire burning on the altar. There was a bittersweet aroma that filled her nostrils. Somehow, there was an unpleasant feeling about this place.

From behind the altar, the high priest walked slowly toward her. His hands were stretched out to her as he said, "I have been waiting for you. My name is Dativas, High Priest of Isis. The spirit of Isis welcomes you. Your husband told me about your condition. Sacrifices and prayers have been given to Isis for over a month. She will open your womb and cause you to be able to conceive. Kneel at the altar, and I will lower the flames of the fire so Isis will abide with you. Close your eyes and pray until dawn."

Aketous inched her way to the altar and knelt. The high priest lowered the flames so low that only a very small light could be seen from the altar. He left her all alone in the dark temple. It was almost obscure darkness.

The tears began to fall from her eyes. She prayed so hard that it seemed her most inner being was going to explode. She wanted a child so desperately. She prayed for hours, crying, travailing with all her thoughts and became exhausted and delirious.

Then did the high priest leap from where he was hidden within and did not fail of enjoying her. She was at his service all the night long, as supposing he was a god. Aketous could not believe what was happening. She wanted to scream, but found her voice paralyzed. She tried to push his body away from her, but he was much too strong.

Horrified at the experience, she lay on the floor near the altar. Was this part of the fertility ritual?

Antibus waited impatiently for his wife a few blocks from the temple. Where was Aketous? Did she not understand that he would be here at sunrise? The sun had already risen high above the mountains. Maybe she was counseling with the high priest. He decided to wait another hour. He would try to find out what was delaying her.

Confused and disoriented, Aketous left the temple before dawn. Her only instinct now was of retreat, to hide, to find a shell of a place.

She considered a safe haven to go to and barricade herself within.

She felt like her mind and body had been violated. Was she in a nightmare with everything spinning out of control? Aketous hurried on her way to the harbor to collect her thoughts. She placed her face in her hands and began to breathe heavily, rubbing the side of her face.

Ignatius arose early for a stroll, as was his custom each morning. The fresh breeze and salty air of the bay felt so good. There would not be many people here this early. The harbor was calm with little activity.

The wind was blowing the white caps of the waves to the piers. He sat at the piers and started to meditate on the good things that the Lord had done in his life.

Aketous covered her face and started to cry. What was happening to her? Had she dreamed it all, or did it really happen? The more she thought about it, the more she wept. It was a horrifying experience.

Was it her mind escaping into a place of non-existence? How was it possible to feel the presence of a god inside you? She ached from the pain of the ordeal. Her eyes could not hold back lamenting.

"How can I render unto the Lord for all His blessings," Ignatius repeated unto himself. It was such a joy to feel the presence of the Lord. Then he heard someone sobbing as though in great pain near him. He could see a beautiful woman dressed in a lilac silk gown trimmed in gold thread. The golden gem combs in her hair held her curls away from her forehead.

"Young lady, are you all right? Could I help you? Have you fallen? What is the problem? Do you need assistance?"

"I do not know. I came here to think. I am not certain why I am here. I have had quite an experience last night. I don't think anyone can understand my situation." She lowered her head, unable to look him in the eyes.

"My precious child, there is a God Who understands all. Yeshua HaMashiach feels for our needs, whether it is pain, sorrow, grief, or whatever disturbs us. There is no problem that He cannot solve. Just trust in Him."

"Who is this God named Yeshua? I do not understand. Who is this One that you are speaking about? Is His statue in the temples of our city? There are hundreds of gods that we pray to every day."

"No, my child, you won't find Him in the temples. He is not a god made with hands, but a living God. He was crucified in Jerusalem on a cross for all of the sins of the world. He became our supreme sacrifice. The grave could not hold Him. He was buried and arose alive on the third day. This man was the Son of God manifested in the flesh. The One the prophets wrote about from the days of old. By praying to Him in His name, God answers our prayers. His name is Jesus to us and Yeshua to the Jews. Whatever your problem is, He will help you. May I pray with you?"

Aketous nodded her head, but could not say anything. She stared at Ignatius as if she was looking through him.

Ignatius felt a strong urgency to touch the throne of Grace. He prayed, "Father, allow me to grab onto the horns of the altar and bring the need before You. I do not understand what it is, but You are the All-Seeing God Who knows all. Comfort her and deliver her from her fears. We trust in You. Give her complete peace in the name of Jesus. Amen."

Aketous felt much better after praying. Ignatius invited her to his house for a prayer meeting the following night. "May I ask what is your name? I do not mean to probe. I will pray for you every morning and night when I seek the Lord. I would like to call out your name before Him."

"My name is Aketous of the house of Antibus, the Senator. I live a short distance to the west beyond those hills. Thank you for praying for me and inviting me to your services. I have someone waiting; I must be on my way."

Ignatius knew where the mansion was. Everyone in the city knew where the estate was located. The tall columns could be seen as far as the seaport. He also could tell she was of nobility when he first saw her by the way she was dressed. Her robe was fringed and embroidered with expensive thread. He felt a burden for her. He did not know at that time how many nights he would carry her name in prayer before God. ➤

Follow the Sign

Chapter 3

The morning sunlight was cutting in from behind his right shoulder streaking across the kitchen table. Erodius had so much work to do today. The silversmith shop had been in his family for several generations. His father had taught him the trade from a lad. The silver was extracted from Galena, a lead ore that had to be imported.

Erodius had been taught all the knowledge of producing quality pieces. The silver could be bent, drawn into wire, and hammered into extremely thin sheets. The fine pieces were much to be desired by those who could afford them. Each piece was polished to a lustrous shine. He was not rich by any means, but he had all that was needed to secure a pleasant lifestyle.

Every day before the workday started, he would recite the Shema from the Torah in Deuteronomy 6:4-9: "Hear, O' Israel, the Lord is our G-d, the Lord is One." Praised be His glorious sovereignty forever and ever. "You shall love the Lord your G-d with all your heart and with all your soul and with all your might. You shall take to heart these words which I command you this day. You shall teach them diligently to your children. You shall repeat them at home and away, when you lie down at night and when you rise up in the morning. You shall bind them as a sign upon your arm, and they shall be a reminder above your eyes. You shall inscribe them on the doorposts of your homes and on the gates of your cities." Each time he recited the Shema he expressed his belief in the one invisible and incomparable G-d. He was linked to all generations of Jews who steadfastly recited these sacred words. He reaffirmed that one G-d is the parent of us all, and all of His children are related by a bond that transcends differences of origin or belief.

Erodius turned south toward Jerusalem to the Holy Temple to pray. He opened his eyes and had a vision of a man standing in the middle of the crossroads near his home. The man took his cane and drew a symbol of a fish in the sand and said, "My family and I have walked a long distance. Could you show us the way to Seleucia?" Erodius saw himself leading the stranger and his family to his home.

Erodius had never had an experience like this before. Everything was vividly clear. Somewhere within the walls of his mind this man's image had been imprinted. The face could not be erased.

The mallet hit hard on the anvil to shape the silver goblet. The etching on the goblet formed a fish-like emblem. Erodius could see the same man's face that he saw in the vision. This was strange and unique. He thought to himself, "I need to rest."

As Erodius left his house, he gently swiped his hand on the Mezuzah that was secure on the doorpost and kissed his fingertips. The G-d of Abraham, Isaac, and Jacob would protect his going and return. As a Jew, this was always done before leaving the house.

Erodius knelt on a rock in order to fill the large container he had carried with water. He had promised his wife that he would bring fresh water from the mountain stream. His hands ached from the day's work as he rested them in the stream. He had completed four quality pieces of silver that day. There were still chores to be done before sundown. The weather looked as if a storm was brewing in the east. It was evident that rain was on the way. He would have to hurry if he made it home without getting drenched.

As he approached the crossroads near his home, he saw a small caravan stalled in the middle of the road. Erodius left his donkey and wagon and walked near the strangers. "What is the problem?" he asked.

The young man had his back turned to Erodius and was marking something in the sand. He turned around and looked face to face with Erodius who had just seen the symbol of the fish drawn in the sand. Erodius was so stunned that he could not speak. This was the face of the man he had seen in his recent vision.

Erodius immediately took the stranger by the hand and said, "My home awaits your visit, for the G-d of Israel has shown me your face and the sign of the fish." ∝ ➤

Follow the Sign

Chapter 4

The terror of the night was forever imbedded in Aketous' mind. Only time could erase the awful memories of forced intimacy that had taken place. She dared not discuss them with Antibus, although she felt she had to talk to someone. She had become a regular at the house prayer meetings. The only time she could feel peace was when she was praying with the Christians. It was her only means of escape. She was now two months with child.

Antibus arrived home from a trip to Rome. The senate had met to discuss two issues regarding inheritance taxes. He was tired from the voyage. Orders were given to the servants to draw his bath. Aketous had everything prepared for her husband's return. Fresh vegetables had been set to cooking in the pots. Olives and almonds had been picked earlier that morning filling the small baskets on the table. She wanted everything to be perfect this evening. As she oversaw the preparations, she thought about how she would give Antibus the news. She knew he wanted a son to carry on the family name. Would he ever suspect the truth about the child?

Antibus entered the dining hall dressed in his striped tunic. He embraced and kissed her gently on the lips. He held out his hand with a green alabaster bottle filled with expensive perfume. He had missed her desperately the last three weeks. Now, the love of his life was in his arms. He held her tight and expressed his love. She was all he could think about.

Aketous looked into his dark, handsome face and melted into his arms. His transparent aqua eyes reflected love as she gazed into them. She stroked her fingers through his thick black hair and said, "I have missed you so much." She took him by the hand, and they walked outside to the garden near the fountain. All was very tranquil when she broke the news. "I will give you a child in six months."

Antibus looked surprised, and then a smile lit his face. He lifted his arms and said, "Praise be to Isis, for she has answered our prayers. Nothing in the Roman Empire could be more important to me than having a child to carry my name."

All the joy she was feeling was drained from her at the mention of Isis. The only thing that was left was pain and a feeling of worthlessness. She could see the joy the child would bring. Still, there was a raw feeling in the pit of her stomach.

After the evening meal, the servants cleaned and left their stations. Antibus could sense that Aketous was not feeling well. She had hardly touched her food. Very little was said in conversation.

Antibus opened the conversation with, "How have you been spending your time here alone?"

"I have been going to meetings with the Christians in Antioch," she answered him.

"Are you sure that is a good idea? What do you know about them?" responded Antibus.

"They are kind and religious people. Many of the Jews in the city worship there. They believe in the God of Abraham, Isaac, and Jacob. Their God sent His Son, Yeshua, to pay for the sins of the world. They claim He is the Messiah. Several of the disciples preached in the synagogue. I don't know if it is a church or a synagogue. However, I really enjoy the services and their company," she replied convincingly. "I am sure the exercise and getting out of the house will do me good. I enjoy the ride near the coast. Maybe you could visit with me sometime?"

"That would probably be impossible at this time. My work has increased drastically over the past two months. I would really like to go with you. Maybe in the future we could go, but now we need to retire for the night.

You really need your rest."

Aketous awoke from a deep sleep frightened from the nightmare about the temple of Isis. She was shaking and crying, "Stop, stop, please stop! You are hurting me." Aketous relived the ordeal in the temple. She saw the silver onyx medallion on his neck as it was pressed against her tense body. Bits and pieces of memories were surfacing from what had happened. She was like a child locked in a dark closet, and the door was slowly being opened.

Antibus awoke to his wife's cries about the onyx medallion against her body. He tried to comfort her. He wiped the perspiration from her brow. "Honey, are you all right?" he asked in a soft voice. "You must have had a bad dream. Just lie here in my arms. Everything will be all right." He pulled her to himself and kissed her on the forehead. It was not long before they fell asleep.

Their eyes opened to the morning sun rising over the mountains. Aketous remembered the stranger at the port and his words about this man called Jesus. Several times in the day she found herself a place to pray. Only God knew what she was feeling. She prayed to Jesus for strength to make it through the day. Prayer meeting would be in the evening.

Antibus left the mansion early in the evening to discuss some urgent matter with a prominent family in the city. He would be home late and told Aketous to be careful going to the prayer meeting.

A short time later, Aketous made her way into the large congregation for the evening meeting. Before sundown, two oil lamps were lit to usher in the Shabbat services. The prayer service was opened with Scripture reading, hymns, and prayer requests. Everyone was lifting their hands and praising the Lord. The presence of the Lord filled the building. They began to worship even louder. Suddenly, some began to speak in unknown tongues. Everyone became extremely quiet. The tongues were heard for several minutes. It was so peaceful and quiet that a leaf could have been heard falling to the floor.

An elderly man began to speak with authority, saying, "Fear not, my child. I am in your midst. I will not leave you comfortless. I know the trouble that has vexed your soul. I was there in the temple of Isis the night of the pain and confusion. I saw the silver onyx medallion. Come unto Me, for I have heard your cry in the secret places, and I will open a door for you.

No one can shut it if you desire to have it opened. You have called on My Name, and I will perform it for you. It is my pleasure to be your one and only God.

There was great silence among all who were at the meeting. Everyone was wondering about the meaning of the message. Aketous began to weep and shake, for she knew that God was speaking to her.

Ignatius instructed the believers about the gifts of the Spirit and how God operated them in the church. He said to them, "Someone has touched the hem of His garment. There is healing and deliverance for them. I do not know who it is, but this person definitely knows the circumstances that have come forth this evening. I feel the movement by the Holy Spirit to pray with you."

Aketous walked to the front of the congregation, knelt, and began to pray. The believers and Ignatius started to pray with her.

They prayed and sought the Lord for a long period of time. It was not long before the Spirit of the Lord was in the midst. Aketous was weeping and repenting of her sins. Others were doing the same. Great joy entered the place of worship. People started speaking in other tongues and worshiping the Lord. Aketous spoke in tongues as the Spirit of the Lord took control. A glow could be seen on her face. She did not know what the words were that were coming out of her mouth, but it was a joyful experience.

Aketous had the feeling that she had been washed whiter than snow. She had experienced this new birth that all the believers were speaking about. There was great joy when Ignatius brought forth the Holy Scrolls. The people danced, and music was played to praise God. Each person touched the Holy Scrolls with their fingertips and brought it to their lips. Ignatius read from the scrolls. Letters were read from the Apostles. Shabbat was complete with Jewish hymns and reciting of the Shema.

After the service, Ignatius spoke to Aketous and asked her to visit him and his family the following day. He would explain what she had experienced from God. There was a need for her to be baptized in water. He wanted her to fully understand what baptism was and what it meant. Aketous felt joy that she had not felt since before her ordeal at the temple of Isis. ➤

Follow the Sign

Chapter 5

The winding sandy road led the way to a villa near the coast. Ignatius and his family followed patiently behind Erodius as they approached the villa. The home was built of dressed stone and was elegantly decorated with beautiful objects imported from abroad. The landscaped terraces caught their eyes as they entered the arched gates that led to the main house.

Erodius secured the way to the door where he met his wife. He introduced her as Ravit. He asked her to help prepare accommodations for their guests. Everyone removed their sandals before entering the house.

Fortunately, Ravit had prepared a large roasted lamb earlier that morning. There was enough to feed both families. They immediately started making bread on the limestone tables. Fresh raisins, pomegranates, figs, and dates were placed in the dessert dishes made of bronze and glass. She was a little ashamed that there was so little on the table. However, it would get them through the unannounced meal.

Lydia and the children were taken to a small house behind the courtyard to freshen up before the evening meal. Titus packed all of their belongings near the central courtyard and waited for instructions on where to unload. The courtyard was paved with expensive flagstone with a large fountain in the center. He waited for Erodius and Ignatius who were visiting in the reception hall for a short while.

Erodius seated his guest on a thick woven mattress supported by wood near the arched window overlooking the seacoast. He spoke nervously, "I have seen your face, and I have been obedient to the vision that has been placed before me. Could you explain who you are and why you are here?"

Ignatius introduced himself as a teacher of the Word of God from Antioch. "I preach the death, burial, and resurrection of our Lord and Savior, Yeshua. Persecution has been laid heavy on the believers of the church. Hundreds have been slaughtered and met their deaths. I have been told that my mother and father were among that number.

"My family and I are in exile. We are fugitives being hunted because of our belief. The Roman authorities will prosecute us to the fullest because of the name we preach."

"I do not understand this," Erodius answered with a troubled look on his face. "Your place of refuge is here, on the south side of my property close to the beach. There, you will find a large cave. The opening is covered with large rocks, palm trees, and brush. I will provide you with water, food, and necessities. I will take you there tomorrow."

The two families were seated at the table. Erodius reached in his pocket and pulled out his *kippah* and placed it on the crown of his head. Each male was given one to wear. Everyone bowed their heads as they heard Erodius say, "Lord God, King of the universe, we exalt You this evening. We give thanks for all that You have done for us this day. We thank You for the fruit of the vine, the grain of the earth, and all that You have placed on our table. Bless it for the nourishment of our bodies as we partake of your goodness. Amen."

Ravit was full of questions about the new guests. She was eager to speak to Erodius alone. Curiosity was about to get the best of her.

Finally, they were alone, as everyone else had retired for the night. Erodius told her about the vision he had the previous night and how G-d had sent Ignatius to the crossroads and drew the sign of the fish in the sand. They lit a lamp and prayed to the G-d of Abraham, Isaac, and Jacob. Erodius thanked G-d for allowing him to be a part of His plan. He remembered how G-d fed the children of Israel in the wilderness and secured them. He told Ravit that G-d must have a special plan for this family. They must do all they can to help hide their identity.

The silvery moon cast its light upon the palm tree near the cave as Ignatius rested against a rock. All was dark inside except for the lamp's soft glow. The children were put to bed early. Ignatius knew that Lydia would have a hard time setting up house in the cave. Who could complain? God had truly given them safety from the enemy. It was very quiet except for the waves rushing onto the shore. Ignatius and Lydia knelt next to each other to pray. Their future was in the hands of the Lord. All they had belonged to Him. It was only borrowed for a short time. They knew that the love of God was more than any worldly possession they had achieved.

Even though his family was out of danger, Ignatius found it hard to sleep. His mind was on the church family at Antioch. The congregation, what was left of it, was without a shepherd. He knew that their faith was strong. He could feel the strength of their prayers. Tomorrow he would send Titus to Antioch to scout out the situation. ➤

Follow the Sign

Chapter 6

A stroll down memory lane was the start of the day as Aketous dressed and combed her hair. Nothing in the past could dictate the mood for the day. Joy had engulfed her in a way that had never seemed possible. The Spirit of the Lord brought liberty. She tried to explain the feelings to Antibus but was at a loss for words. All he said was, "Anything that makes you happy makes me happy."

Antibus left for the city early that morning. Aketous ate her breakfast alone and was feeling somewhat queasy. A little fig preserves on a piece of flat bread was all she would eat. All of the excitement had robbed her of any appetite. As she nibbled on the last bite, she heard a voice from the entrance of the courtyard.

"My lady, your carriage is ready," said the servant with his head bowed. Aketous draped a shawl around her shoulders and walked to the gate in the front of the mansion. She seated herself on the pillows in the carriage. The driver was given the directions to the house of Ignatius on the outskirts of Antioch.

The drive along the coast seemed to renew her strength and caused the nausea to diminish. Aketous could almost taste the salt in the air as it blew upon her face with a cooling effect in the morning sunlight.

Lydia heard a knock at the gate. She walked to the front of the house and saw Aketous smiling with a glow on her face. She invited her in and sent Titus to get Ignatius.

"It is so nice for you to visit us today," said Lydia. "Won't you please come in and be seated."

"Thank you," responded Aketous, smiling as she entered the doorway. "My name is Aketous. The man of God asked me to come here today. I believe he wanted to explain some of the beliefs and baptism."

"The bishop is at the church. He will be back soon. Have a seat, and I will prepare us some refreshments," responded Lydia. "We are so glad to have you be a part of our congregation. We have so much work to do. There is always room for another soldier in the Lord's army."

"Lydia, I'm home," Ignatius called out softly. "Titus told me that we have a guest. Oh, hello, Aketous. How are you?" Ignatius stated smiling.

"I'm fine, thank you. I need to talk with you and your wife. My life seems so different now. I feel so clean inside for God has forgiven me of my sins. The guilt from the past is still present. I will forever deal with it. May I confide in you and your wife?"

"It is certain, that is why we are here," replied Ignatius. "I assure you that anything reported to us will not leave this room. Whatever is told to us in secret will remain that way."

"When you first saw me at the piers that morning three months ago, something had happened to me that night." Aketous trembled as she spoke. "I was unable to conceive. My husband arranged an appointment with the high priest of Isis to fertilize my womb. I never dreamed that the ordeal would haunt me. I prayed for hours at the altar. I was exhausted and alone in the temple with little light. I felt hands on my body. My clothes were removed, and I could not escape. His movements pressed the onyx medallion he wore against my body. I felt like my insides were being ripped apart. It was a long time that I remained paralyzed with fear on the temple floor. Feeling violated, I dressed and left the temple. You found me that morning at the piers. That is why I was so distressed. I still have nightmares about what happened. Now I am with child to deliver in six months. I am very confused and ashamed," sighed Aketous.

"Words have reached my ears of many evil things that have happened in the temple from many of my members. Dativas, the high priest, has done many things that are an abomination in the sight of our God. I am sure the Lord will deal with him according to the way he deals with others," stated Ignatius disdainfully.

Follow the Sign

Chapter 7

"Travel to Antioch by night," were the last words that Titus received from Ignatius three days before. The trip would take much planning and complete secrecy. Every day would bring his family closer to the truth of what had taken place.

The chilly darkness brought horror to the mind of Titus as he walked carefully through the ashes of what used to be a church. Blood stains were present on the rubble of what used to be pillars that supported the structure of the walls. Only in his mind could he conceive the terror that had taken place where he was now standing. Titus bent down on his knees and wept silently and began to pray. He heard his name being called, "Titus, Titus, I can't believe it is really you," echoed a voice in the distance.

Titus lifted his head and could see the outline of a man walking straight toward him. It was Abednego, one of the deacons of the church. He said, "Follow me. We are in great danger. The ground that we walk on is cursed by the innocent blood of the saints. God Almighty will repay the avengers for the wrong that has taken place. Now come. We must leave immediately, for the danger is great. Follow me down the trail behind the church to the marsh. There we can talk freely."

After reaching the clearing near the edge of the marsh. Abednego began to speak of the ordeal that had transpired and changed the lives of the believers in Antioch. Abednego hung his head and said, "The terror that we have feared has come upon us. The story that I am about to tell will be told by generations after generations in the future. It all began just after your Uncle left for his trip to Laodicea. The young maiden named Aketous, the senator's wife who has been coming to services with us, was somehow in the midst of the scandal. It was told that Antibus went to talk to the high priest of Isis. He was told that the Christians had put a curse on her, and the baby would die. The high priest told Antibus that he would take care of the matter. He said the Christians were to blame for all the problems in the area, and they were nothing more than an abomination in the sight of the gods.

Antibus immediately made way to the Governor's house. There, he brought with him two witnesses to testify of the curse that was made known at the meeting of the Christians. The Governor called for two battalions of soldiers to rid Antioch of the Christians. It was about four days later when the sun was down that we came together at the church for prayer."

At that moment, Abednego paused in his speech, trying bravely to compose himself. At length, he continued with his story. "In the midst of the prayer service, the door was swung open, and the pits of hell came upon us. A General read charges against the Christians. The soldiers drew their swords and began the slaughter."

The voice of Abednego began to tremble, and Titus laid a comforting hand upon his shoulder. Abednego drew a shaky breath and began to speak again. "Men, women, and children had nowhere to go. The screams and cries of torture were all over the building. I was kneeling and praying on the east side of the congregation. Someone threw something and hit me on the head. I lost consciousness. When I came to myself, the building was on fire. I made my way through the dead bodies. My tunic was covered with blood. I don't know how I made it out of the burning building alive. The next morning, I found myself in the forest behind the church. I was unable to move for several hours. My head began to clear from all the smoke I had inhaled. I was the only one at the service who had survived. There are others in the city who did not come to the service for various reasons that night. The soldiers began a massive search for Christians all over Antioch. Many families were killed the following day. I have been hiding since the slaughter. It is hard to trust anyone here. People are running scared all over the city.

My dear brother, what are we to do?"

"We heard of the massive slaughter while traveling on the road," replied Titus, trying to hold back the tears. "My uncle has sent me here to find out information and report back to him. He is staying with someone near the coast. It appears we are all fugitives. It will soon be dark enough to travel. We must make way before morning light, for fear of being caught by the soldiers. Ignatius awaits our return." ➤

Follow the Sign

Chapter 8

Antibus spoke softly and said, "I refuse to travel and leave this house until I know you are completely well. It has been over a week, and you still have those terrible nightmares. The doctor said that you must get complete rest. He has mixed us some herbs and said to apply them to the soreness of your abdomen and to keep you cool. My mother will assist and care for your needs."

Somehow, the feeling of guilt was weighing heavily on her mind as Aketous' voice spoke softly saying; "Oh, Antibus, I am so sorry for causing so much trouble. I have not felt the baby move inside me for many days. What awaits me in my hour of distress? I can't bear to think of losing this gift of life. My heart cries out for need of relief from this misery."

"My love, you must get some rest," whispered Antibus. "You must close your eyes and allow your mind to be at ease, for you are only making matters worse," as he gently wiped her forehead with a damp cloth.

"Antibus, my Antibus. In the prison walls of my mind, there must be rest. Sit next to me, for I need to tell you about the temple of Isis and the nightmares," said Aketous.

"What are you talking about?" responded Antibus very puzzled.

"I tried to do what the priest told me to do. It was so dark, and I prayed so hard. Someone violated me in front of the altar. I can still remember feeling the silver onyx medallion pressing against my body. For months, I thought it was a god or some sort of ritual. It was so unclean, and I was so confused and in pain. Someone at the church in Antioch spoke my ordeal, and the bishop has prayed for me. Why has this happened to me? My love, please forgive me. I am so scared. I do not know what to do," spoke Aketous, weeping uncontrollably.

Antibus put his arms around her and was about to speak when his mother walked into the room.

"Antibus, three days ago, I placed three statues of Isis with three cuttings of rosemary in the window sill knowing that a full moon would be approaching us soon. May the gods hear my cry, and come to our aid," said Antibus' mother. "Many years ago, when I was about to give birth to my second child, your father's sister told me to do so. After this, someone must light incense of myrrh in the temple."

"I will leave for the city now to speak to the high priest, Dativas, about the incense. I am sure he will assist me in doing so," said Antibus, eager to help the situation. Reaching for his cloak and turban, he told one of the servants to prepare his ride to the Temple of Isis immediately.

Without hesitation, he left the room.

The overcast skies filtered the rays of the hot sun. Antibus' eyes were fixed on Dativas as he was standing on the left side of the temple door talking to a young girl.

"Dativas, may I have a few words with you?" asked Antibus. "Just a moment," responded Dativas as he excused himself and walked toward Antibus. "Antibus, what could I do for you today?" spoke Dativas politely.

"Many months ago, my wife came to the temple for help. She was visited by the spirit of Isis and her womb was opened to conceive a child. Do you remember our meeting?" asked Antibus. "I remember it very clearly," said Dativas. The Senator answered, "She has been with child and is very ill. At times, she seems to be confused or troubled about the ordeal. She told me that someone violated her in the temple that night. Would you elaborate on what exactly took place?"

"Incense and special prayers were given to Isis to help her conceive. I left the temple in order for her to experience the presence of Isis in a way only a woman could. I know nothing of what happened after I left her that evening. I was told that several Christian men were seen entering the temple before dawn the next morning. I will have this investigated to the fullest. It is hard to believe that this could have occurred in such a sacred place. The priest managed to appear shocked. ➤

Follow the Sign

Chapter 9

The small fishing boat set sail for Laodicea from the harbor. It was propelled by oars and single sails. The two attendants were exhausted from running along the rocky coast to the fishing piers. Abednego wiped the sweat from his brow and said, "I'm so glad I thought about the boat that belongs to Jonah. It is so hard to realize that he and his family were among the masses that were slaughtered."

"The Lord has prepared our way of escape. I have never seen so many soldiers in Antioch. Every crossroad in the city was heavily guarded, with no one leaving without being questioned. I have never seen so much fear in the people," stated Titus. "The journey by boat will take a full day. We should reach an inlet close to the city. We can hide the boat and walk along the beach till we reach the house of Erodius," he added, just about out of breath.

"We can thank the good Lord it is cloudy, for the sun won't beam its rays upon us and blister our bodies. With only one pitcher of water, we can make it by sundown if the current keeps pushing us to the south," spoke Abednego as he got into a comfortable position.

"Let us pray to the Lord to guide our vessel in the right direction and fill our sail to maximum capacity," said Titus as he took Abednego by the hand and began to pray. They rowed the oars until the wind filled the sail and pushed them fast upon the glistening water.

The palms were swaying in the breeze as the afternoon sun was sinking over the horizon. All was tranquil and calm inside the cave as Ignatius lifted his hands and began to pray. "Oh, heavenly Father, God Almighty, my heart is heavy with grief. I know not Your plan for this hour. News has not reached my ears of what is left in the city. My family has no home to return to. Titus has been gone for many days, and still I have no information on the families left in Antioch. What am I to do? My heart aches for Your Presence, and my mind needs rest. Oh, Ancient of Days, I plead the blood of Yeshua, your Son, who gave life for us all. Please hear the prayers of your servant in the name of Yeshua."

"Praise the Lord. They are all right," spoke Ignatius, with his face slowly drooping to his chest. "Thank God for their return," he whispered to himself. As he lifted his head, he saw Titus and Abednego walking down the path looking straight at him. He could tell by the look in their eyes that all was not well. Abednego greeted his bishop with a hug. The silence and the expression on their faces told of the grief they were experiencing. Abednego said, "Why has this happened to us? Your mother, father, and so many families slaughtered. How can it be that I have survived?" he sobbed uncontrollably.

"In times like this, it is hard not to question God. He still has everything in control. We must trust him completely. He will not leave us to be devoured by the enemy," replied Ignatius embracing him.

"There are about one hundred and fifty Christians left in Antioch. The Romans are hunting them as we speak. The roads are not safe to travel. What are we to do?" asked Abednego.

Ignatius answered firmly, "We must pray. God will show us the way. The Lord made a way of escape for Paul and Silas in jail at midnight. It is just as dark for us at this time. There is nothing impossible for Him. We will put our trust in Him, for the God of Israel never slumbers or sleeps." ➤

Follow the Sign

Chapter 10

Erodius lit the lamp saying, "Gracious G-d, thank You for the privilege of ushering in another Shabbat of rest and peace. The heavens and the earth, and all they contain, were complete by the seventh day. G-d had finished the work that He had been doing. G-d blessed the seventh day and sanctified it because of it. He ceased from all His work of creation." As the lamp continued to burn, he began to quote the Kiddush saying, "Praised are You, Lord, our G-d, King of the Universe. Creator of the fruit of the vine. Praised are You, Lord our G-d, King of the Universe, who has taught us the way of holiness through the Mitzvot. Lovingly, You have favored us with the gift of Your Holy Shabbat as our inheritance. A reminder of creation, first among the sacred days that recall the Exodus from Egypt. You have chosen us of all peoples for Your service. You have given us a sacred purpose in life. In loving favor, You, Lord, have given us Your Holy Shabbat as a heritage. Praised are You, O Lord, Who hallows the Shabbat."

Erodius opened the ark and lifted the Torah from its resting place. He walked the Torah around the room. Every eye was on the word of G-d. Each person touched the Torah with their fingers and brought it to their lips. Great joy was present. The *parashah* was read as the family listened to every word that was spoken. With ending remarks, Erodius said, "Praised are You, O Lord, our G-d of our ancestors. G-d of Abraham, G-d of Isaac, and G-d of Jacob, great, mighty, awesome G-d, supreme over all. You are abundantly kind, Creator of all. Remembering the pity of our ancestors, You will lovingly bring redemption to their children's children. You are the King who helps, delivers, and protects. Praised are You, O Lord, Shield of Abraham."

As the light glowed in the house, all eyes were glued to the Torah. Ravit and the children sat in complete reverence as every word was spoken. The three boys had *kippahs* on the crowns of their heads in respect to the authority of being taught by a teacher on Shabbat. With the ending of the reading of the Torah, Erodius said, "With a full heart, I thank you for the strength which I was granted to overcome its difficulties. I ask Your blessings for the week that lies ahead. Grant health and contentment and protection for my family and new friends. Help us to strengthen each other with gentle words and acts of kindness. Be gracious to Your people, Israel, O Lord, our G-d. Lovingly accept their prayers. May our worship ever be acceptable to You. May our eyes behold Your merciful return to Zion. Praise to You, O Lord, Who restored His presence to Zion."

"Our day of rest is complete, and the Lord has blessed us this week," said Ravit, as she lay still on the bed, exhausted from the day. I have grain and some other things that our visitors may need. If you have time tomorrow, would you load them into the wagon and deliver them?"

"Before going to the shop for work, I can drive by the cave with the wagons," replied Erodius. "I know that they will appreciate all that we can give them. My heart goes out to this family. I believe they are good religious people. Somehow, it is strange to hear them say that they worship the one and true G-d and that He is one for all my life. My ancestors taught the Jewish people the same words. This is the thing that has separated us from the World. These people are different and express a love for G-d that hasn't been seen in this region. Show me in the morning where you have the food and supplies stored. I will load them. He quoted the Shema saying, "Hear, O Israel, the Lord our G-d, He is one." And he fell fast asleep.

Sometime about the third hour, a gusting wind began to blow. A large tree limb was rubbing against the roof of the house making a disturbing noise. Erodius awoke to the sound of rustling in the wind. He arose and walked to the window to see what was making the noise. There, along the path to the beach, he saw people traveling with goods. They were being led by Ignatius and a young man with the symbol of the fish above their heads. He sat down and was stunned by the vision of the symbol of the fish. He began to pray, "Almighty G-d of Israel, G-d of the prophets, my eyes are not just to see things that you have showed me. This man and these people, what are they to do with me? My G-d, what is this sign of the fish?"

Erodius prayed the remainder of the night. Pouring out his soul to the G-d of Israel. All he knew was that he had to speak to Ignatius about the vision and the meaning.

Bright and early that morning, Ravit started breakfast for the family. She was preparing date and raisin rolls, covered with cinnamon and almonds. Erodius was bent down picking up the last basket of grain to be loaded into the wagon and did not hear Ravit talking to him. Raising her voice, she asked with concern, "Are you feeling well today? Is something bothering you?"

"Ravit, G-d has given me another vision about these people and the sign of the fish. I have no idea what it is about. This happened in the early hours of the morning. I felt troubled and a sense of fear for these people. My hands are stretched out to help in any way I can."

"I am sure you will do what you can. Do you think you need to go and speak to the Rabbi in Seleucia?" asked Ravit.

"I have been praying whether to tell the Rabbi about these people, but somehow it does not seem necessary at this time," responded Erodius.

"I have baked two loaves of raisin and date bread," Ravit said. "They are in the small basket wrapped in white cloth. Please take them to the Christian family."

Ignatius was carrying two jugs of water to the cave when he saw a wagon coming down the seashore. From a distance, he could make out the figure of Erodius. He was driving toward the entrance of the cave. As he stepped out of the wagon, Erodius could hear Ignatius call to him, "Shalom!" He returned the greeting and invited his new friend into the cave. Upon entering, they saw Abednego. Ignatius introduced him as a deacon of the Antioch church. Erodius stared transfixed as he realized this was the man he had seen with the sign of the fish over his head in his vision.

"It has been five days since our visit. I came to bring some food and supplies for your family. The purpose of my visit is to tell you of my experience in the early morning hours. I have received another vision from G-d. My eyes have seen you and this man leading a group of people with the sign of a fish above your heads. I do not know the meaning of all of this."

"I know the meaning of the vision and the mission that God has for us," said Ignatius. "We will help the believers out of Antioch by using the sign of the fish. Titus and Dativas have told me the details of the slaughter. There are many Christian families left in Antioch. They must flee the swords of the Romans. If they don't escape, death is imminent. We must fast and pray for the guiding of the Spirit. The Lord is our provider and protector. He will keep us in His arms of safety. Let us seek His council."

"I will pray for you and the other Christians left at Antioch. If there is anything I can do to help the situation, please feel free to speak to me. There are some supplies in the wagon. We can unload them near the cave," said Erodius. ➤

Follow the Sign

Chapter 11

Thick black smoke rose high above the trees blocking the view of the ocean. Antibus stood looking from the balcony of the mansion. "I wonder what has taken place in the city. There is smoke everywhere," he noted.

"I don't know," said his mother as she walked to the edge of the balcony to get a better view. "Something dreadful must have happened to create so much smoke. I think you need to find out what is happening in the city. Why don't you go ahead and see what has happened? Aketous has had a peaceful night. I gave her something to help her sleep. I will stay here with her until you return."

It was almost noon when Antibus and four servants arrived in the city square. There were soldiers everywhere. At the crossroads near his home, a roadblock was set up, and two soldiers asked him if any of his servants were Christians. He told them, "No!" and found himself puzzled by the question he had been asked. He told them he was a Senator of Rome, and they drove the team of horses through the roadblock.

Near the large fountains and statues in the city square, people gathered to discuss the ordeal that had transpired the previous night. The high priest, Dativas, was speaking to the people, saying, "These heretics need to die. They have caused our crops to fail and have stolen money from the temple.

They have also gathered together to put curses on the citizens of Antioch. I have heard that they poisoned the wells on the outskirts of the city. It pleases me to say that Rome has done its job during the night. May death fall on the rest of them."

As Dativas finished speaking, Antibus could not take his eyes off the silver onyx medallion swaying from side to side of his robe. Without hesitation, Antibus drew his sword shouting, "Liar, liar!" Leaping forward, he pierced Dativas just below the medallion. Blood flowed from the chest of the priest as his lifeless body fell to the ground. The crowd began to step back as screams were heard. An elderly man shouted, "He has killed the high priest of Isis! Arrest him, arrest him!" Two soldiers made their way through the mass of confusion and grabbed Antibus. An officer yelled, "Bind him, and lock him in the ship!"

All the way to the ship, Antibus was shouting, "I am the Senator of Rome, and I'll have your head for this." The soldiers laughed at him in disbelief as they escorted him to the piers.

A large, tall man in armor started to calm the multitude of people down. He spoke as one having authority, saying, "We are here to provide assistance to the Governor for the problems that have erupted in this area. A death sentence has been placed on all Christians in Antioch. Anyone knowing the names and whereabouts of the accused should give that information to the authorities. There will be stations set up at various locations in the city for people to register. Those refusing to comply with rules thus stated will suffer the consequences." As soon as he finished speaking, the crowd dispersed, as many sought the nearest station in order to register.

The servants spoke to several officials of the city to get the full story. They found out that hundreds of Christians had been killed. The church was burned to the ground. The scent of death was everywhere. *Was this the way the high priest had handled the matter?* Aketous must not know about the slaughter. The Christians had put a spell on her. They were responsible for their own punishments.

After arriving home, the servants spoke to Antibus' mother, telling her about the arrest of her son. ➤

Follow the Sign

Chapter 12

The long trip home was over. Two men lowered the anchor into the water near the north side of the harbor. Judah was so excited, for he had not laid eyes on this brother in twelve years. This was the year of Jubilee, the time when all land would be given back to its original owner without payment. All cultivated land was to be fallowed. He had come not only for a visit, but to discuss the future of inherited land deeded back to his family. It had been thirty years since their father had rented the land in Megiddo to a wealthy family from Jerusalem to plant olive trees. Now the land was to be given back to his family. There would be so many details to work out. He was thrilled to discuss his plans with his brothers.

Erodius had fasted and prayed for a day and a half. He was still burdened down with grief for his new friends at the cave and their family at Antioch. He told his wife, "Where are all these people going to go? I fear for the safety of the children. My heart is heavy, and I am so burdened for these people."

"It was so many years ago when we left Jerusalem. We were pushed out of the city for something that was out of our control. We came here to make a new start. Our G-d has supplied for us. I believe that all things are according to His plan. Surely, He has a plan for these people," spoke Ravit as she gently placed her hands on his shoulders for support.

Out of the arched window, Erodius could see three men approaching the entrance to his home. All of a sudden, he could hear the words, "Shalom, shalom." He could not believe his eyes. It was his brother, Judah, whom he had not seen in so many years. As the three men came closer to the house, Erodius made his way to the front of the house shouting, "Shalom, shalom."

"I can't believe my eyes," said Erodius, hugging Judah as hard as he could. "It's been such a long time. I am so glad to see you."

"My brother, I don't know when the Lord has given me such joy. Seeing your face lifts my spirit higher than the clouds. When I saw you near the house, my heart leapt within me. This is such a pleasant surprise," said Judah.

"How did you find the house?" asked Erodius.

"That was easy. I asked the first Jew I saw in Seleucia for directions. Jews always know where another Jew lives," laughed Judah.

Judah walked forward and acknowledged Ravit's presence saying, "Ravit, it is so good to see you. You have not changed a bit. My brother is so fortunate to have you. Look at this fine home. Are the beams overlaid with gold or silver?"

"Judah, you have truly surprised us. It is so good to see you. To tell you the truth, the beams in this house are covered with wood," said Ravit, as they all laughed together.

"The eldest son can help your servants unload and show them where they can find the stables. Come on in and rest, for I know you are tired from your trip. We will have food this evening, and we can catch up on what has happened over the years since I have been away." Erodius placed his hand on Judah's shoulder and showed him to the guest quarters.

After a large dinner and catching up on the years apart, Judah focused on Erodius and said, "I have some family business to discuss with you."

"What could it be? I thought all that was settled when we left Jerusalem years ago after father's death," said Erodius, puzzled.

"There is a small matter with the estate that we have overlooked," replied Judah.

"What is it?" asked Erodius.

"Many years ago, Father had a piece of land inherited by him from his grandfather. It was in a place called Megiddo. At this time, he had many debts and leased the land to his brother. This is the year of Jubilee. Remember, every fifty years, the land returns to its original owner," said Judah.

Nodding his head, Erodius said, "Yes, I understand."

"You are the eldest son, my brother. That gives you the first right to the inheritance of the land. I have visited the site. The land is very fertile, with palm trees, pomegranates, barley, wheat fields, and a large olive orchard," said Judah.

Hours later, Erodius spoke to Ravit about the inheritance and the possible move. They knelt in prayer together, with Erodius saying, "G-d of Abraham, Isaac, and Jacob, Your sovereignty shall reign forever. As far as the east is from the west, your Kingdom shall be established. We look to Your direction," prayed Erodius.

Sleep was far from Erodius, as his mind raced with so many thoughts. He finally drifted off to sleep before dawn. In a heavy sleep, he dreamed about many people following the fish sign to Israel, leading to an oasis in the desert called Megiddo.

Early in the morning, Erodius threw a sheep blanket over his horse to pad the ride to the beach. At the mouth of the cave, he could see Ignatius and two other men seated around a campfire.

"Shalom, shalom," greeted Erodius, smiling at Ignatius and the two other men with him.

Small talk was exchanged as Ignatius introduced the two visitors to him saying, "Remember my nephew, Titus, and this is one of the deacons from the Church of Antioch. They have just arrived with devastating news of the slaughter," said Ignatius.

"I am full of grief of the things I have been told. My brother arrived here last night on business in Seleucia. He spoke to me concerning a tract of land in Israel that is in need of workers to develop a new settlement. This is an inheritance left to me by my father. I will need good workers and skilled artisans to develop this investment. Is it possible that you and the Christians of your congregation could relocate with me to this new development?" asked Erodius.

Ignatius looked at Erodius speechless. His eyes were full of tears. Erodius then told Ignatius of the dream and the sign of the fish leading the way for the Christians.

"The Lord is with us, for He has prepared our way of escape," Ignatius stated with a broken voice.

"We must have a plan to get the Christians out of Antioch. I can speak to my brother about giving them voyage to Israel. I am sure it will be no problem. The cave can be used as a refugee camp until they are ready to leave," Erodius stated.

"Deliver the word to the Christians in Antioch about a plan of exodus. I can send Abednego to spread the word. The sign of the fish can be posted to show the way. All of the details can be worked out," said Ignatius.

Prayer without ceasing was all that could be done at this time. Ignatius, Titus, and Abednego prayed with all their mind, soul, and strength as Erodius mounted his horse and trotted off in the distance.

In the early hours of the morning, just before dawn, Ignatius walked out of the cave for some fresh air. He left Titus and Abednego on their knees praying heavily in deep concentration. He was exhausted and weak. He sat on a large rock and could hear the waves rushing into the shoreline. His mind was not clearly on the things around him. Ignatius was having trouble with his sight adjusting to the darkness of the night. He lifted his head and looked toward the black sky, staring into the heavens and said, "Lord Jesus, we are desperate to know what to do. Many lives have been lost in Antioch. So many more lives are in danger at this moment. We plead Your blood that was shed on Calvary. Thy will be done. Please hear our cries and show us Your will. In the name of Jesus, I pray." In the sky, he saw a vision of a fish on fire with its tail curved, pointing toward Israel. ➤

Follow the Sign

Chapter 13

The servants arrived at the senator's house after sunset. Troubled and confused, the chief servant walked into the main room and asked Antibus' mother to meet him in the courtyard. "I have something urgent to speak to you about in private."

Antibus' mother left Aketous with one of the maids and followed the servant to the courtyard. "Where is Antibus?" she asked.

"There have been hundreds of Christians slaughtered in Antioch. The priest of Isis was speaking to the people about the incident when Antibus went wild. He drew his sword and killed the high priest. The Romans arrested Antibus and locked him on their ship. I guess they will take him to Rome," replied the servant.

Antibus' mother placed three fingers to her lips and was unable to speak. "What are we to do?" asked the servant.

Pulling herself together, Antibus' mother replied, "The senator has a good friend named Anteninus who lives near the harbor. Make way immediately and inform him of everything that has happened. Tell him Antibus needs his help. His influence with the authorities will help us. I do not want a word about this spoken to Aketous. She is in no condition to deal with it."

Without hesitation, the chief servant left for the house of Anteninus. It would take him over an hour to reach the estate. Tired and exhausted, he walked slowly on the rocky path that led to the estate.

It was after midnight when Anteninus heard a heavy knock at the main gate. He arose and sent one of the servants to investigate the matter. Quick words were exchanged, and they made their way up the faded marble steps. "I am the chief servant at the house of Antibus, the senator," said the disturbed man.

"What is your business at this late hour?" asked Anteninus.

"I have come with terrible news of the senator. His mother has sent me here. The senator has been arrested for the murder of the High Priest of Isis," said the chief servant. He recounted all that had transpired just hours earlier.

Anteninus dressed as fast as he could while telling servants to make his carriage ready. If he could make it to port before the ship left, he could talk to the authorities.

The short ride to the port seemed to take longer than usual. He left his carriage and walked along the piers with no ship in sight. The ship had already set sail for Rome. ➤

Follow the Sign

Chapter 14

It was early in the morning when Aketous awoke and decided to go for a short walk. Her body was stiff from so much rest. She tiptoed out of the room to keep from waking her mother-in-law, who was sleeping soundly.

Aketous approached the courtyard and sat beneath the begonias.

She could hear voices coming from near the fountain. The servants were talking, "This house is plagued with misfortune," said the slim elder servant to the younger one.

"I can't believe that the senator was arrested for murder of the High Priest of Isis. Last night the chief servant was sent to the house of Anteninus for help. I heard that the senator is being held on a ship in the harbor. There were many people who saw him draw his sword and thrust it into Dativas. I believe he has gone mad," said the younger servant.

Aketous stood to her feet, stunned by the tragic news of her husband. She raced to the house as fast as her feet could move her pregnant body. Stepping upon the top step near the threshold she tripped and rolled down the concrete steps screaming in pain. Aketous laid on her stomach trying to catch her breath. The pain was unbearable.

The two servants came to her rescue. They lifted her and entered the house. Her voice was convincing evidence of the excruciating pain.

One of the servants began to shout saying, "Someone go and get the midwife. I believe her time has come."

Aketous' mother-in-law shouted from the second floor and said, "Bring her to my room, now. We will need water and blankets."

Moments later, Aketous was lying on her back with the midwife telling her to push as she bit on a piece of leather. Sweat was pouring off her forehead. Every contraction made her body ache to the fullest degree of pain. She screamed louder as the pain intensified. The midwife told her to hold her hand and push with all of her might on the next contraction. Aketous grabbed her hand as the pain increased. She pushed with all her strength. The baby made its way into the hands of the midwife. She cut the umbilical cord and rubbed it with sea salt. The new baby boy was turning blue. She tapped the baby and no sound was heard. She tried to get the baby to breathe. The breath of life was not present. The baby was stillborn. Aketous' mother-in-law stared at the baby with tears streaming down her face. All at once, she said, "Oh, my God. Oh, my God."

The midwife wrapped the stillborn baby and laid it on the marble floor. A few seconds later a faint cry was heard. The mother-in-law picked up the newborn and unwrapped the clothing. The voice of the baby was heard in the silent room.

Moments later, Aketous was holding her new baby boy and thanking God for the miracle.

Aketous looked at the right side of the room across the arch to view three statues with incense burning in front of them. Her mother-in-law walked to the statues, chanting in a slow whisper, to teraphim, her family private idols.

Lifting her right hand, Aketous thanked her new God, the God of the Christians for the precious gift of life. The Lord had given life to her and to the newborn. ➤

Follow the Sign

Chapter 15

The ship arrived at port with the battalion of soldiers surrounding the senator. He was being held for the death of the High Priest of Isis. It would be a quick trial because there were so many witnesses to the murder.

Antibus was delirious to the fact of what he had done. His anger drove him to a place of revenge. The image of the medallion around the high priest's neck would forever be an imprint in his mind. His violent behavior had taken its toll on his family. What would Aketous do now that he would be put in prison waiting for trial!

The tears rolled down his cheeks as he thought of all that had happened. If only he could go back and filter out the problem. He felt like the gods had abandoned him. He knew Roman law. His persecutors would have a quick trial to appease the tension of the people. The abeyance would come in a few days, only to usher in the ruling.

Antibus remembered riding in a chariot from the seaport to the main parts of the city to begin his work with the senate. This time he was shackled and tied around the neck. He was being marched to his destination. He raised his head, looking to the sky searching for some sign of Zeus or Athena. Is there any god that would come to his aid?

The sun was beating down on Antibus, and he felt the weight of the load he was carrying. Two soldiers stripped him of his tunic, down to his bare chest. They threw him behind the iron bars with just his inner garments being exposed. The place was filthy and unbearable. There were rats in the corner of the cell, running along the side of the wall with large black bugs crawling above them. The dirt and foul scent made him gag. He made his way to the corner of the cell and vomited. He continued vomiting until there was nothing left in his body. He began to dry heave, his body aching as he gagged.

The other men from the adjoining cells watched without saying a word while Antibus lay on the dirt floor.

Several hours later, a guard opened the door and threw a bucket of water at Antibus to wash the dried vomit from his aching body. ➤

Follow the Sign

Chapter 16

Erodius arrived with his family at the entrance of the cave. There was a small table with two small lamps, the Torah, bread, wine, and a large bowl with a pitcher of water. Ravit whispered to her husband and said, "I don't see anything different about this Shabbat service. It looks like a traditional Shabbat service. I wonder what is so different about these Christians.

Everyone spoke to each other with the Hebrew words "Shabbat Shalom." They all sat near the table and watched with eagerness. All of the men were given *yamakas* to place on the crown of their heads.

Erodius explained that they were worn in service to reverence G-d as the one in authority to us all. They were all called *kippahs*.

The olive oil lamps were lit before sundown, and Ravit issued in the Kiddush for the Shabbat eve. She spoke with a veil over her head saying, "Praised are You, O Lord, our G-d, King of the universe who has taught us the way of holiness through the Mizot. Lovingly You have favored us with the gift of Your Holy Shabbat as our inheritance, a reminder of creation, first among the sacred days which recall the Exodus from Egypt. You have chosen us of all people for Your services. You have given us a sacred purpose in life and in loving favor. You have given us Your holy Shabbat as a heritage.

Praised are You, O Lord, Who hallows the Shabbat.

Several Jewish songs were sung about deliverance from Egypt. The Torah was brought out of its casing and was marched around so everyone could touch it and bring their fingertips to their lips. The Torah was placed on the table and unscrolled so the passages could be read.

Erodius began to read the *parashah* portion of the Torah. Readings from the prophets were also read. He began by saying that a branch will emerge from the trunk of Jessie. A shoot will grow from his roots. The spirit of Adonai will rest on him. The spirit of understanding, council, power, the spirit of knowledge, and fearing Adonai. He will judge by what His eyes see or decide by what His ears hear. He will judge the impoverished justly. He will decide fairly for the humble of the land. He will strike the land with a rod from his mouth and slay the wicked with a breath from His lips. Justice will be the belt around His waist. Faithfulness the sash around His hips. The wolf will lie down with the lamb. The leopard will lie down with the kid. They will not hurt or destroy anywhere on My holy mountain. The earth will be as full of knowledge of Adonai as the water covering the sea.

After the reading of the ancient scrolls, they were closed and placed in a box that was called an ark. Ignatius took the liberty to explain the Scriptures that were read. He said, "Adonai has spoken about the branch that will grow. I am here to say today that the branch has come to us as promised out of the horns of Jessie. Also, the house of David that was spoken by the Prophet Isaiah many years ago. Not so many years ago in Jerusalem. He has secured His place as the Messiah. He shed his blood and died for all. He rose on the third day to bring salvation to the lost. His name is Yeshua HaMashiach in Hebrew.

The preacher spoke with bold authority about this Messiah. The words seemed to fall upon the ears and penetrate the hearts. Bread and wine was served as remembrance of liberation from Egypt. He spoke of the body and blood of the Messiah. The blood was applied to the doorposts of our hearts to liberate us. The hands were washed as an offering to Adonai. The Shabbat ended with psalms and praises to Adonai and Yeshua.

On the way home, Erodius and Ravit spoke about the words they heard and the warm feeling they felt in the service. Never had they experienced the moving of the Spirit in such a great way. The shalom they felt was so powerful. ➤

Follow the Sign

Chapter 17

Judah had unloaded the ship of its cargo. He would return to Israel to Megiddo to visit the new settlement with his brother Erodius.

Erodius was not too happy to leave his new friends at the cave.

There was still so much friction in Antioch. The Roman guards were still arresting Christians. Roads were still blocked. For several days he was able to get some supplies and food for his new friends at the cave. They would have to make the best of the situation. Lydia was told to send two servants with fresh water daily for Ignatius and his family.

Titus was as strong as a bull and able to help out with unloading the water. He spoke to the servants about the trouble in Antioch. They were told about the problems in the area concerning the Christians.

Everything was a secret. After much prayer and fasting, a decision had been reached. Ignatius and Titus would leave at dawn in the boat to retrieve some of the Christians.

Ignatius gathered the family together in prayer saying, "We are grateful for the ability to worship. We are grateful for the day the Almighty is preparing for us all. As You delivered the children of Israel, out of the hands of Pharaoh, so may You redeem all of Your children out of oppression. We pray in the name of Yeshua. ➤

Follow the Sign

Chapter 18

Aketous awoke from a deep sleep and asked for the baby. Her newborn was placed on her chest to feed. As she positioned the baby, she noticed a very small birthmark on the left side of the infant's upper leg. She could not believe her eyes. Antibus had the same birthmark on the same side of his leg. Tears welled up in her eyes and ran down her cheeks. She knew in her heart that Yeshua had given her a son of Antibus.

Aketous' mother-in-law saw a difference in her and asked, "What has happened that makes you smile?" Aketous told her the complete story and showed her the birthmark. Her mother-in-law knew the birthmark was the same as was on her son.

Aketous testified of Yeshua and how He had saved her life. He had given her hope. She told her about the cross and the power of the resurrection. The Spirit of God engulfed their room as they prayed.

They were both touched by God's presence in a special way.

Late in the afternoon, her mother-in-law sent one of the servants to gather all of the idols and incense in the house. She told them to destroy the idols near a small hill on the north side of the property. She felt a fear of having them in the house.

At the same time, Antenius was gathering all of the evidence he could find against the Priest of Isis. Every lead was important to free his best friend. He knew that time was short, and he had to gather witnesses of the wrong doing.

At the edge of the harbor, there were many rooms to store imports coming into the country. Anteninus made his way without being noticed by anyone to the back side of the storage areas. Three men who had duties in the temple walked in and began to talk about the riches that had been obtained through the years by Dativas, the high priest. They spoke of how they had helped to deceive the people and felt that since Dativas was dead, they had a right to claim all of the loot. They spoke of their plan to move all of the gold and precious items within two days. Everything would be loaded and sent to Ephesus to be stored in the temple of Athenia. One of the men spoke of how he saw Dativas attack the senator's wife and what a good deed fell on them. Antibus had killed the high priest, and now they were set for life.

After hearing this conversation, Anteninus had all of the evidence he needed to take care of freeing his friend. He would relay what he had heard to the captain of the battalion. They could set a trap to catch the thieves with the loot. Time was very precious. He had to move swiftly with the new information. ➤

Follow the Sign

Chapter 19

It was about a day's journey from the seaport to Megiddo. They saw two caravans of camels traveling on the Kings Highway headed south.

Judah was very familiar with the trade system along the Mediterranean Coast. He explained to Erodius about how they traveled so far to trade goods back home in Egypt.

Close to the end of the day they reached Megiddo. They traveled a short distance to **Armageddon**, a small settlement with lush vegetation and a large oasis with palm trees in the distance.

The donkeys were unloaded, and camp was made ready for the night. The desert heat would be cooling, and the coolness of the night would be invading them. A small fire was built to give a little warmth and to brew some tea.

Erodius had seen some beautiful places in Israel years ago, but this place could outshine them all. What beauty to the eyes! Surely this was what his ancestors referred to as "the land of milk and honey." The bright colors of the landscape were breathtaking. *What a beautiful place to raise a family,* he thought to himself.

Early in the morning, Judah began to tour the estate with Erodius and the workers. They saw the olive orchards, pomegranate trees, date palms, and an old settlement with a large building in the center. The building was used as a synagogue many years ago. Their first reaction was that this could be the place for the Christians to worship. Erodius was overwhelmed with all that he had seen in the special place.

After a long and exciting day, Erodius placed his *tallit* over his shoulders and his *kippah* on the crown of his head. The fringes with the blue thread lay close to his lower waist. He thought so much about his ancestors being led out of Egypt by Moses and Pharaoh's army being defeated at the Red Sea. Adonai always delivered His people when they cried out to Him. The Lord God of Israel was their refuge. He had fought their battles and given them the victory.

Erodius prayed several Jewish prayers and meditated on the goodness of Adonai. His mind traveled back in time to his childhood. He remembered his father telling him about a king who owned a large, beautiful, pure diamond. The king was justly proud of the diamond, for there was none equal anywhere. One day, the diamond accidentally sustained a deep scratch. The king called in the most skilled diamond cutters. He offered them a great reward if they could remove the imperfection from his jewel. No one could repair the blemish. The king was sorely distressed. After some time, a gifted craftsman came to the king and promised to make the rare diamond even more beautiful. It would be better than before the mishap. The king was impressed by his confidence and entrusted his stone into his care. The man kept his word. With superb artistry, he engraved a lovely rosebud around the imperfection, using the scratch to make the stem. Erodius thought to himself, *Life's bruises have wounded the Christians, and I can use the scratches to etch a portrait of beauty and charm for them. They shall live here and have a new start, for the G-d of Israel is with them!* ➤

Follow the Sign

Chapter 20

The main servant dashed through the door of the mansion shouting, "There are soldiers coming up the hill. They will be here soon. The carriage is ready. Gather a few things, and we will leave on the back road before they come. We can travel along the road near the coast."

Aketous and her mother-in-law grabbed a pile of clothes and the baby. They moved as fast as they could to the back of the mansion. They all climbed into the carriage. Though it was only a short time, it seemed to take forever.

Three furlongs down the road, the driver realized that they were coming to a crossroad. It led to town and would be blocked with Roman soldiers. He knew an old, abandoned road that went into the forest to the coast. He took a left onto the old road and raced along the path.

After two furlongs, they stopped a few minutes to rest. They had made it to the outskirts of the cliff near the inlet. They were frightened and scared of what might happen to them if the Roman soldiers spotted their carriage. Aketous began to call on the name of Yeshua for help. "Which way do we go?" They heard a voice yelling. It was Ignatius and Titus.

They were hiding on the other side of the rocks behind the low brush of bushes. The boat was hidden from view at the edge of the inlet by the beach.

Ignatius lifted his eyes to heaven and prayed, "Oh, Lord, our God, on this sacred day, we thank You for redeeming our friends from the Roman soldiers. We place our souls within the palms of Your hands. Praised are You, Lord God, King of the universe. You have enabled us to escape the hands of the enemy. Send your angels to shield us from all of the wrath that Rome has for us." ➤

Follow the Sign

Chapter 21

Two soldiers escorted Anteninus to a small room where the captain of the battalion was seated. One of the soldiers said in a rough voice, "This is Anteninus of Antioch. He has some information of utmost importance for you to hear."

The captain rose to his feet and said, "Leave us alone to talk." The soldier left the room with Anteninus standing facing the captain.

The captain said, "What can I do for you today? What is so important that I have to be taken from my duties?"

Anteninus told the captain all that he had heard about the loot, and the rape. He also told the captain about the years of stealing from the exports and how the high priest was involved in the entire scandal. Fear gripped him as silence fell among them.

The captain called for five soldiers to make way to the harbor to look for any sign of a ship being loaded. The description of the three men were given to the soldiers. Anteninus was told to wait in the captain's quarters until an investigation was completed.

Anteninus thought much about his friend. He well knew of the harshness and punishment the Roman soldiers could inflict on Antibus. Surely the captain would get the evidence to free his friend. ➤

Follow the Sign

Chapter 22

Erodius and Judah arrived in port at Antioch close to noon. They had set a time to load the Christians onto the ship in two weeks. The ship would set sail at midnight. There would be little light from the moon to detect any movement around the inlet.

Judah placed his arm around his brother's shoulders and said, "Father would have loved the excitement that you have gotten yourself into. May the Lord G-d of Abraham shield you all from the Romans.

"Please, before you go home, spend some time with the Rabbi at the synagogue. He will assist you in prayer. I have two deliveries to make to Rhodes. G-d will give me wind in my sail to return to complete the task."

Erodius watched his brother drift out of the port in the large ship riding high upon the waves. In the midst of all the excitement, he had a good visit with his brother. He remembered their time together as children in Israel. *Could it be that G-d was calling him home? What would Ravit think of his new plans? What would the Rabbi think about his feelings for these Gentiles?* His mind was racing for the answers. If he left now, he could meet with the Rabbi and discuss his new plans. The sun was still high. In one hour, he could make it to the synagogue.

The servants were told to take Erodius' belongings home. News would be sent to Ravit of this urgent business with the Rabbi. It would be about dark before his return home.

Erodius and a servant mounted their beasts of burden at the edge of the port. He could see two men packing a large fish they had caught.

Many people were following them to view the fish. His mind pushed to the vision he had received of the fish only a short time ago into a reality state of existence. The sign of the fish ⌒× would lead the Christians out of the hands of the Romans to a new home in Israel. ➤

Follow the Sign

Chapter 23

The short ride in the boat washed them upon the small beach on the rugged coastline. Ignatius knew from the look of terror in their eyes why they were in a state of confusion.

Lydia met the two women and the infant with arms opened wide. She helped pack their few possessions. Everyone was speechless and lost for words.

Ignatius spoke in a loud voice, lifted his hands, and started to pray, "Father, God Almighty, we are in Your care. Thank you for our protection. In the midst of this trial of tribulation, we call on Your help to secure us in this place of refuge. Our church has been demolished, and many of our brothers and sisters have lost their lives for being Christians. Still, there are members of the church in hiding. We remember all that was done to Israel in their hour of tribulation. The blood on the doorposts gave them protection from the death of the firstborn. Their sacrifice of blood shielded them from death. They left Egypt the next morning free. Father, shield us by the blood of Your son, Yeshua. We claim His blood for our deliverance."

His hands were moved to his side as he asked everyone to join hands and pray in unity for help and deliverance from the Roman soldiers.

Erodius walked from behind the small crowd and took Ignatius by the hand. Everyone joined by holding someone's hand. They all prayed together, crying and pouring out their hearts before God.

After the group prayer meeting was over, Erodius spoke to Ignatius about relocating the Christians to Israel. He told him of his visit with the Rabbi at the synagogue. Everyone was told about the vision of the fish and the Christians. The Rabbi told him that a stranger could join them and become a part of the congregation if they desired. It was in their law to allow this to happen. The last word that the Rabbi said was, "Life is given to us by Adonai. Adonai will give life to all who seek Him. Place our letter חי with the sign of the fish ⊂< for them to follow. Explain to the Christians that the letter means 'life' in Hebrew."

Erodius and Ignatius agreed to have all the Christians who came from Antioch to meet near the cave. Ravit would make *kippahs* and *tallits* for the men to wear. This would help to deceive the Roman soldiers if they came near. They could say they were gathering to celebrate the feast of Pesach. They would celebrate the first in two weeks near the cave. They would then board the ship at midnight after Pesach. All of the Christians would follow the sign of the fish, ⊂< looking at its tail for direction. They would also look for the letter חי for "life" in Hebrew. This fish and Hebrew letter would be placed at all trails from Antioch to the coast and ending at the cave. The unseen hand of Adonai would guide them safely. ➤

Follow the Sign

Chapter 24

A short, slender man fell on his knees and began to pray, asking Yeshua to give him strength to stand in this time of need. He cried and raised his hands as though his God was next to him. He prayed for a long time. His face became radiant as he continued to pray. His sorrow became praise to his God.

Antibus heard this man and watched him very closely. The Spirit of God came into the cell, and peace settled in their midst. He could do nothing or say anything, only bowing his head and feeling something he had never felt before. He asked the question, "Who is this God you are praying to?"

In response to the question, the man answered, saying, "His name is Yeshua. He was born in Bethlehem, Israel. He preached a message of salvation to all that would hear Him. The message that He preached still lives in the hearts of the believers. We are all called 'Christians'."

"Could you tell me about this man? My wife started going to their meetings a short while go," stated Antibus.

"Love for one another is the most important thing He taught. Many miracles were done by this Man. He turned water into wine. He healed the blind, the deaf, and raised the dead. The people followed Him to Jerusalem. Many were witnesses to the events that took place there on Golgotha. This is where Yeshua, some call Him Jesus, died on the execution stake. He suffered and died at the hands of the Roman soldiers and the Jewish political figures of the day. Before He died, He made intercession for all sinners.

His blood was shed for the ransom of all people of that day and every generation to come. He entered into the tabernacle and became High Priest and sacrifice. Everything that could possibly be done for mankind was achieved that day. The veil was rent from top to bottom as He entered into the Holy of Holies. God's mercy came down to earth and pardoned the sins of all who receive Him. His death brought forth victory for all. His body was placed in a tomb. The grave could not hold Him. Three days later, He arose from the dead back to life. He was seen and heard by His disciples and a vast number of people all around Jerusalem. They saw His nail-pierced hands and feet. He spoke to His disciples on a certain mountain. His disciples saw God lift him into the Heavens. He did not leave them comfortless. They were told by Jesus to go to Jerusalem to pray and wait. He told them He would come again. He gave His disciples the power of the Holy Spirit. All of this was prophesied by the prophets of old and became a testament. For He was the Torah robed in flesh and became the New Covenant."

"How can I believe in such a man? Will He hear me? I just committed something terrible," spoke Antibus.

"There was a man named John, known as the baptizer, who preached and prophesied about Yeshua. He told the people to repent of their sins. He immersed them in water to baptize them, a type of entering into His death and resurrection. The people were told to prepare the way of the Lord and to make straight the paths of our God according to the way that the Lord God commanded you to go, in order that He may give you rest. The ancestors of old were told to remove the other gods from among them and make straight your heart to the Lord God of Israel. We believe with our heart and make an open confession to Yeshua to forgive us of our sins. Our sins separate us from God. The only way to come clean before God is through this man named Yeshua. He was the Son of God who taketh away the sins of the world. His blood that was shed on the execution stake covers our sins and saves us. To receive this salvation, one only has to believe on Him."

"Could you help me believe and pray to this Man, Yeshua? I am full of fear. Help me find the way to Him," cried Antibus in a soft voice.

The two men knelt and prayed to Yeshua for salvation as the Spirit of God entered the prison cell. ➤

Follow the Sign

Chapter 25

As the Word began to spread like wildfire among the Christians, Erodius knew he had to get everything prepared for Pesach, the Jewish Passover. It was going to happen in only four days. Several days before, he decided to have Passover at home. All leavened items were removed from the home. These included all breads and cakes that contained yeast. Preparation began with a thorough cleaning by Ravit, culminating in a ceremonial search for leaven, called Bedikat Khameytz. Their hearts had to be prepared for the Passover Seder. Traditions were taught in each generation that they must consider themselves freed from Egypt. As they were to prepare for this experience of personal redemption, they knew to be far from the leaven of sin hidden within their hearts.

The Passover Haggadah was the telling of the story that had been told for thousands of years. It was from slavery to freedom, from despair to hope, from darkness to light. It truly was the greatness of their external truth of His involvement with His people.

The Seder plates would have to be prepared for the Passover meal holding the ceremonial items of the Passover. There would be bitter herbs, a roasted egg, a sweet apple mixture, parsley, and a lamb shank bone. Curious thing, yet all part of the telling. It would have to be set according to the diagram he would draw to give his helpers instructions to prepare the plates. It would look like this …

SEDER PLATE

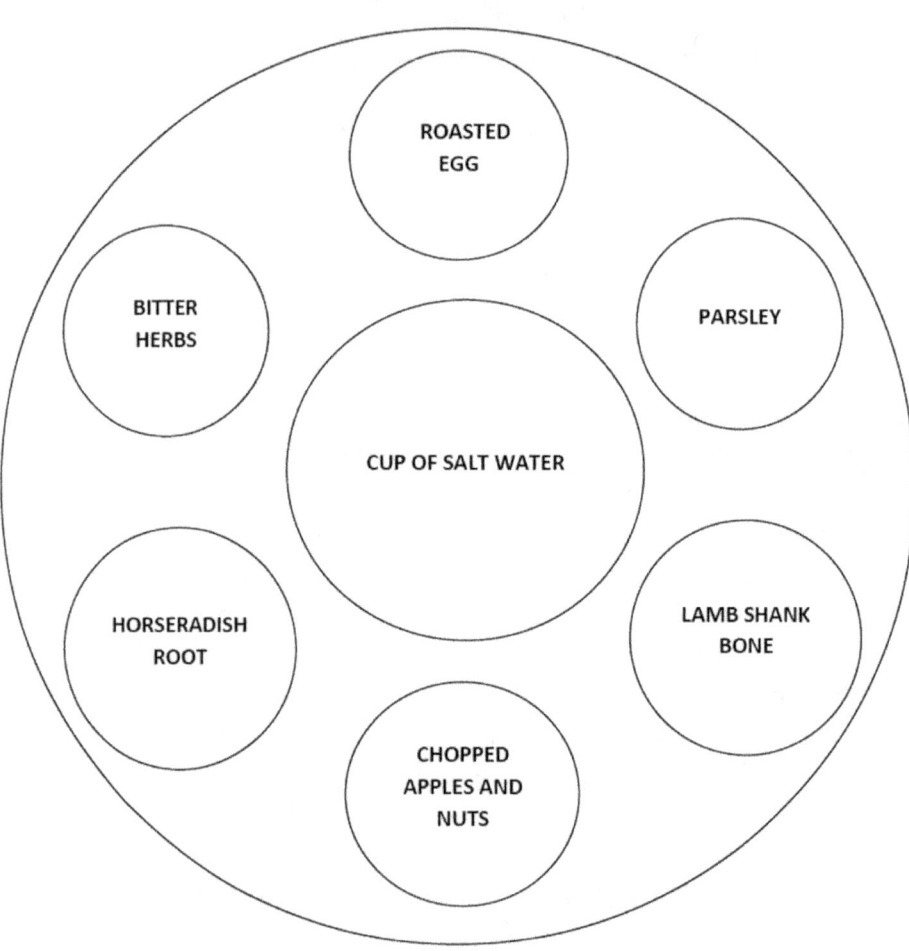

Follow the Sign

Chapter 26

The moon dipped behind a large cloud with a faint glow overlooking the cave. The ocean's current would push the small boat toward the back side of Antioch. It was four hours until daylight. The two men had a mission to complete. Every trail, path, and road had to have the sign of the fish ⊂⊱ etched in rock to lead the way to the cave near the cove.

This secret code would guide the passage to safety for the Christians.

The early morning tide beached the boat near the ruins of the church toward the back of the property. The beaten path could not be seen, for morning twilight was still an hour away. After walking a short distance from the church, Ignatius motioned for Abednego to lie down in a grassy area near the path under a tree. As soon as light appeared, they would start mapping a trail for survivors to follow, leading them back to the cave. The sign of the fish ⊂⊱ with its tail in a half circle pointed the way to the old forgotten road along the coast.

The fresh breeze blew the leaves on the tree softly and continually. The birds began to chirp as twilight started to force light from behind the clouds. Ignatius looked up into the heavens and prayed silently while Abednego slept, holding onto the bag of provisions.

Just as the sun was coming up on the eastern horizon, the two men were startled by the whisper of a voice saying, "Brother Ignatius, Brother

Ignatius! It is Brother Waqas from the church. I saw you from the cliffs as you entered the inlet with your boat. I worked myself down as fast as I could. You are not safe here. Come, follow me to the ridge. There is a large thicket on the other side. There are six families hiding in the brush. Quietly take your bags, and let's go."

Waqas led the way through a rough ravine. The light was starting to take the darkness as they came up on a large ridge covered with brush and a few trees in the distance. There, they saw the families sleeping near a large opening toward the south side of the ridge.

The men were awakened by Ignatius. They were told of the plan for the exodus to take place in three days. He passed out *kippahs* and *tallits*. He told the men to wear the *kippahs* on the crowns of their heads and a *tallit* over their shoulders. Travel on the old forgotten road to the cave near the cove. He told them to mark the way at each path and all along the way with the sign of the fish. ⌒⌒ It should be written in the sand and etched in the rocks for others to see. If, by chance, they saw anybody, they were to say they were making a short pilgrimage to celebrate the Pesach, the Jewish Holiday. Spread the word to all Christians in the area of Antioch that are still here. ➤

Follow the Sign

Chapter 27

Tired and exhausted, Aketous and her mother-in-law sat near the entrance of the cave on a blanket with the newborn baby. They were uncertain of all that was taking place around them. A wagon pulled up with supplies and water to be unloaded. Three men unloaded everything and put it into the cave.

Several new families had made their way in the dark and arrived in the early morning. The men had *kippahs* and *tallits* and looked to be Jewish, but also familiar. One of the men began to speak, telling about seeing the sign of the fish ⟨⟩ along the way to guide them to the cave. At the sound of his voice, Aketous recognized him from the church services at Antioch. The story began to spread around the camp of their escape from the hands of the Roman soldiers.

Fires were started to cook food to feed the families. They were hungry and very thirsty.

Aketous heard that Waqas had etched and drew the sign of the fish with the cross, and two Hebrew letters as instructed. Not only was the crossroads marked, but every trail near the church, the old abandoned road, and all roads around Antioch.

"I need to help," said Aketous' mother-in-law. "I can't just sit here waiting when I can be of use. Your place is here with the baby while I boil water to make a soup. I will go through the provisions that were unloaded and get started." ➤

Follow the Sign

Chapter 28

For four days, the Christian families gathered near the cave for hope of refuge. The sun was hiding itself behind the horizon when the blast of the shofar sounded. Every male had a *Yakama* on the crown of his head. A *tallit* with fringes and dangling threads of blue were draped around his shoulders.

Two oil lamps glowed near a small table with a Torah scroll opened as Erodius spoke to the congregation, with Ignatius at his side.

"Our G-d and G-d of our ancestors, may the rays of these festival lamps cast their glow upon the earth. May they bring the radiance of Your light to all that dwell in darkness. Bless our home with the spirit of this festival. Bless our dear ones with the light of Your Spirit. Praised are You, Lord, our G-d, King of the universe, Who has taught us the way of holiness through the Mitzvot and enjoyed upon us the kindling of the festival lighting," spoke Erodius.

"May the brightness of these lamps banish all gloom, anxiety, and care from my heart and the hearts of my loved ones. May this Shabbat bring us peace and serenity, joy, and rest. Keep aglow within us, O G-d, the spirit of gratitude for Your many blessings so that we may know the sweet taste of contentment and the rich harvest of sharing. Kindle in our home a deep love for one another, for our people, and all Your children. Teach us true freedom, O G-d of freedom, Who revealed Yourself with these words: "I am the Lord Your G-d who took you out of the land of Egypt, out of the house of bondage. Many are the slaveries still afflicting humanity, ignorance, poverty, and fear. Lust for power, wealth, and fame. Only those who place on their shoulders with their own hands the yoke of Torah, are free to carry its life-giving waters to a parched barren land.

The Haggadah was read that set forth the order of the Passover Seder. Many words were spoken about Passover and how it commemorated the liberation of the Israeli slaves from Egypt.

The Seder plates were placed near the beach. Each family sat near their plate and went through the explanation of the food and what it represented to the exodus so many years ago in Egypt. Each family ate of the Seder plate and thanked God for deliverance from Pharaoh.

At the end of eating the bitter herbs and roasted lamb bone, the last plague was told about the instructions of putting the blood of an animal on their doorpost so death would not enter their home on the last plague. The horror that had visited Egypt that night. Death was everywhere, even in the palace. Pharaoh's first born was dead.

Erodius told them that death had to come in order to bring deliverance and freedom.

The Passover had gripped the heart of every believer who was present. Ignatius placed his violin in his hand and began to play a joyful melody. Erodius and his family began to dance with excitement as they formed a circle. It was not long before all were joining them in the dance. They were praising G-d for their deliverance.

The Passover Festival of Pesach lasted for five hours. ➤

Follow the Sign

Chapter 29

It was getting late. After the last family had left the ravine, Waqas started etching the last sign of the fish ☓ on the side of a large bolder.

Abednego and Ignatius set out to place the sign all around Antioch. Waqas' job was to do the same. Every crossroad around the burnt church was marked.

The walk to the cave would take a while. Waqas knew he would be safe. While etching a rock, four furlongs from the church, he saw three Roman guards. They questioned him and wanted to know what a Jew was doing at the crossroad. He told them that he was giving directions for a Jewish Festival. The guards gave him orders to be off the road by sundown.

The last crossroad was about thirty minutes away. As Waqas was walking, he felt a stinging pain in his left ankle. It became so unbearable that he sat on the road and took off his sandal. The pain was excruciating.

His foot began to swell. The sting on the side of his ankle revealed a redness, numbness, and tingling in the area. A scorpion's venom had invaded his body. His muscles began twitching, and he began to experience unusual head, neck, and eye movements. The pain was so severe that he started drooling and sweating as he lay in a fetal position. All of a sudden, he became nauseated and vomited. His heart rate accelerated, and he felt paralyzed. He remained lying on the ground for a long time.

The sun had set, and the darkness of the night was fully visible to his eyes. Waqas lifted himself up from the ground. He tried to walk and felt very weak. All he could think about was making it to the cave in time to leave with the others. So much time had been lost. ➤

Follow the Sign

Chapter 30

In the early hours of the morning, Anteninus and the captain of the battalion left the ship at Rome. A chariot was delivered to the port as they began the ride to the prison.

The captain walked through the gates as the guards opened them. They positioned themselves at attention. At the third gate, the captain said, "You wait here. I will go and release Antibus and bring him to you." They were armed and were led slowly to another room.

Antibus felt like his life was coming to an end. He prayed as he was walking to the large room. The march seemed endless as the door was slowly opened. He heard his name called out loudly.

"Antibus, you are coming home with me," shouted Anteninus.

Antibus was shocked to see his friend standing there. He was speechless as they hugged each other tightly. His first words were asking about his wife, Aketous. Anteninus told him that they would talk when they reached the bathhouse. There, he could clean, shave, and change his dirty clothes. Much rest would be needed for his aching body.

At the bathhouse, the warm water was soothing, and he received something to eat. Antibus was told about the burning of the Christian church in Antioch. So many lost their lives. As far as he knew, Aketous was fine at the mansion waiting for his return.

Tomorrow, they would leave early on a small ship to Antioch. ➤

Follow the Sign

Chapter 31

Two small boats beached near the cove as Judah made his way to the cave where Erodius was speaking. "Go with my brother, board the ship, for God has provided refuge for you in Israel. Children and women, gather your things and go first. All will have passage. We will take many trips to have everyone on the ship. We will all leave together. The God of Israel has given you refuge from our enemy this day. Put your full trust in Him," spoke Erodius.

Titus and Abednego started helping the women and children into the boats. When the boats were full, Judah and three men jumped in slowly as they were pushed out to sea. On the south side of the cove the ship was anchored and ready to receive the passengers.

Judah knew it was going to take at least five loads to get everyone on the ship. The passengers had very limited provisions with them. A few had bundles of clothes.

On the last load, Ignatius put out the fires as he prepared himself to walk to the beach. One hundred twenty-five Christians were going to Israel.

Erodius hugged his friend, and they prayed together. They thanked Hashem for the exodus to the new village in Israel.

All was quiet as the last ship pushed out to sea. Erodius was waving when he spotted a man limping toward him. It was Waqas. Erodius motioned for the ship to return to pick up the last passenger. Two men got out of the boat and helped Waqas. It was well after midnight when the ship pulled anchor, and the sails were set to push the ship to its destination.

The plan had worked perfectly. Everyone was buoyant as the large ship began to ride the waves to their new home. The sign of the fish ⚯ had led them to safety. Surely, it would be told by future generations.

The Romans were defeated by the unseen hands, and victory was given to the remaining residual of the church of Antioch. ➤

Follow the Sign

Chapter 32

The small wooden ship anchored near the port as Antibus and Anteninus made their way through a crowd of fisherman who had gathered near the docks. On the north side of the docks, there was a stable where they could rent two horses to ride home.

Two hours later, they arrived at the mansion. Antibus opened the door and shouted, "Aketous, Aketous," but no one answered. "Mother, I am home," but no reply. There was no one home. The place looked like it had been looted. Dishes and vases were broken. Furniture was in pieces. *Someone has destroyed our home.*

He searched in every room trying to find someone. The house was empty. The whole mansion was in a state of total disorder.

Anteninus went to the stable to search. He began yelling, "Is anyone there?"

Someone stepped from behind a stack of hay and responded, "I'm the only one left here!" It was the head servant of the house.

They were coming out of the stable when Antibus was walking into the door. "Oh, my God, what has happened," uttered Antibus. The head servant told Antibus he received word that the Roman soldiers were coming to the mansion. He loaded his mother, Aketous, and the infant into the carriage and drove them toward the old abandoned road to outrun the soldiers.

There, they met up with Ignatius and Titus. They took them to the house of Erodius the Jew. I have heard this man has helped all of the Christians in Antioch. He is their friend.

Antibus told the head servant to gather all the other servants to watch the home, for he would return after he found Aketous, his mother, and the infant. The two friends left in gallop on the horses to the house of Erodius. They were desperate to find information about Aketous. ➤

Follow the Sign

Chapter 33

The sea was calm as the sails were full of wind pushing the ship forward. The G-d of Israel had placed His hands on the remaining Christians of Antioch.

Ignatius gathered everyone together to remember those who had lost their lives in Antioch. His heart felt deep grief knowing that his mother and father were among the slaughtered. He was sorry he could not be with them.

It was early morning when everyone on board began to stir. Children were looking out on the vast scenery that was so spectacular. They had never seen such a beautiful sight.

All along the side of the ship, passengers were lined up eager to reach the new land.

Ignatius gathered everyone together. They were told that the voyage would take two and a half days to reach Israel if the winds were strong. A short morning service was conducted.

Titus and Abednego made their way to the ship's hull and brought loads of food to be given to the families. The male of each house was given enough food to feed his household. Erodius had supplied ample provisions for the trip.

At sundown, Ignatius was invited to dine with Judah in the captain's quarters. The two men sat down at the table. Judah was wearing a *kippah* and handed one to Ignatius to place on the crown of his head. Judah prayed in Hebrew, saying, "Baruch ata Adonai, Eloheynin melch ha-olam ha-motzi lehem min ha-aretz."

Judah could tell that his new friend did not know what he said. He translated the prayer: "Praised are You, Lord, our God, King of the universe, Who brings forth bread from the earth."

The evening meal was enjoyed as the two new friends talked about the new land and the plan that was about to be put into action as soon as they unloaded everyone. ➤

Follow the Sign

Chapter 34

Antibus and Anteninus trotted their horses at a driven pace on the abandoned road. Every cross section had a sign of a fish etched on a rock, sometimes drawn in the sand. They could see a large home on top of a cliff near the cove.

Antibus said, "That is the home of Erodius, the Jew. I had him make some silver goblets years ago."

As they approached the gate, they were met with a servant asking them why they were there. Antibus told him he was the husband of Aketous, and he was looking for her. The last word that he heard of her was that she had gone to the house of Erodius, the Jew.

The servant told Antibus that his master had gone on a trip and would not return soon. If he wanted more information he could speak to the Rabbi in Antioch. The servant was not able to give out private information.

The ride back to Antioch was very long for many reasons. Things were racing in his troubled mind. Was she alright? How was the baby? He had no answers, only the thoughts of them fleeing the Roman guards.

"You are coming home with me to my house," Anteninus stated. "There is no place for you to stay tonight. It will be late when we get to Antioch. You can see the Rabbi tomorrow." Antibus nodded in agreement.

In the early hours of the morning, Antibus could not sleep and prayed to Yeshua HaMashiach for the safety of his family. He prayed, "I have given my life to You. You delivered me out of prison and the hands of the Romans. I am your servant, my Lord. Hear my plea unto You this morning, for I am desperate to find Aketous. My heart aches for knowledge of her and her whereabouts. Give me favor with the Rabbi. Help me, O Lord."

After a short breakfast with Anteninus, he mounted his horse and set out to find the Rabbi. ➤

Follow the Sign

⟵⟶

Chapter 35

High in the sky, up above the ship, seagulls were circling the ship as it anchored near the port. Everyone waited anxiously. Titus and Abednego helped the women and the children board the small boats that would take them to the sandy shore.

After all of the men had been taken to shore, the crew unloaded the food and necessities that were sent by Erodius.

Ignatius told the men to pack the food and other provisions. The Christians followed Ignatius and walked at a slow pace for six hours until they saw in the distance a fertile place in the desert. It was filled with palm trees and a large pool of water. The pool was fed by a spring and would be clean for drinking. The tremendous oasis awaited their arrival.

The large group of Christians waded into the edge of the water to cool their scorching feet from the desert heat. There, they rested as Ignatius spoke to them, saying, "We will make camp here. Men, gather palm branches and reeds to burn."

After the fires were lit, everyone gathered to pray and give thanks to God for their safety. Ignatius told them that this was the land of Erodius' ancestors. He would be joining them shortly. Just as God had led the children of Israel out of bondage, he made a way for them out of Antioch. The Christians worshipped and praised the Lord.

Ignatius lay down beside of his wife, Lydia. Their children were gazing at the stars and soon drifted off to sleep. All was peaceful and tranquil, free from disturbances. The Christians were safe and now began to rest.

In the early hours before dawn, Aketous awoke. She thought she heard the voice of Antibus crying out to her. She began to weep and cried out to God silently, not to awaken anyone. "G-d, help me. I cannot go on. Life is not worth living without Antibus. My pain is more than I can carry. I have no means of support for his child. O God, please hear me. What am I to do?" she spoke softly. "I can see the water rushing and trying to take life from me." ➤

Follow the Sign

Chapter 36

There was a knock at the gate of the synagogue. A young boy was asked by a stranger to get the Rabbi. The door to the synagogue was opened as the Rabbi walked to the gate. The two men's eyes made contact as greetings were exchanged.

"I have come with an urgent matter, Rabbi," said Antibus.

"Shalom, what could I do for you today, Senator?" spoke the Rabbi.

"A short while ago, my wife, mother, and baby were driving down the old abandoned road and were met by Ignatius. They were taken to the property of Erodius, the Jew. He is not in trouble for anything. I just need to speak with him concerning my family," spoke Antibus in a low voice.

"Come to the edge of the barley fields on the back side of the city. Look for two large trees with a boulder in the center of them. I will meet you there. You will find me waiting. It is a good place to discuss the matter," replied the Rabbi.

Antibus followed the instructions and finally found the large barley fields. He had never been there before. He looked for the two trees the Rabbi had spoken about in their earlier conversation. He searched on both sides of the fields. He could barely see the two trees and the boulder from the great distance.

The Rabbi was waiting patiently to talk to Antibus as he walked to the meeting place.

"Now I will give you the information that you seek," said the Rabbi. "Erodius has safely transported the Christians to a settlement in Israel called Armageddon. You will find your family there. They are safe from the Romans. God has preserved them for a special work.

"Erodius shares in their vision. After he told me of the vision he had of the sign of the fish, I myself have no doubt. Go now, and you will find them there. May the God of Abraham, God of Isaac, and God of Jacob send His Shalom with you." ➤

Follow the Sign

Epilogue

The small ship was on course to Israel. Antibus had spent two days looking for someone to take him to Armageddon. He was able to rent the small ship with four sailors to bring him to get his wife, mother, and child.

Late in the afternoon, clouds began to develop toward the south. The waves were very choppy, and white caps were racing on the tops of the waves. Lightning was striking, and the wind began to blow. The main sail was taken down as the helpless ship swayed from side to side. Water came crashing onto the deck. The small ship hit the rocks and started to break apart.

Antibus found himself in the violent sea floating on a board that broke away from the sinking ship. He was drifting in the dark open sea with waves as high as hills. After a long and fearful night, he lost the board.

Antibus started sinking and crying out to Yeshua. His life was about to be over. He was out of strength and going down for the last time. The depth of the sea was about to claim him. Suddenly, a vision of Aketous appeared before him. He felt something hitting his body. Large fins were circling his sinking body …

The story continues in Book II of the "Torah To Calvary" Series.

Cast of Characters

Abednego
Young male member of the Church at Antioch.

Aketous
Wife of Antibus.

Antibus
The Senator living near Antioch. Husband of Aketous.

Anteninus
The friend of Senator Antibus.

Erodius
Jewish leader in the community of Antioch. Husband of Ravit.

G-d
The spelling of God in Hebrew.

Ignatius
Pastor at the Church in Antioch. Husband of Lydia.

Judah
Brother of Erodius.

Lydia
Wife of Ignatius who was Pastor at the Church in Antioch.

Ravit
Wife of Erodius, the Jewish leader in Antioch.

Waqas
Young Christian male who etched and drew the sign of the fish for the Christians to follow.

Glossary

Abeyance
a state of temporary disuse or suspension.
Adonai
"The Great I Am" in Hebrew.
Antioch
First church where believers were called "Christians."
Armageddon
Ancient city in Megiddo, Israel, about 90 km north of Jerusalem.
Battalions
A large body of troops ready for battle.
Bendekat Khameytz
A ceremonial search for leaven in a Jewish home before Passover.
Flagstone
Flat stone used for paving slabs or walkways.
Jubilee
50th year. Leviticus 25:1-4.
Kings Highway
Ancient thoroughfare that connected Syria and the Gulf of Aqaba. Mentioned in the Old Testament. It is one of the worlds' oldest communication routes.
Kiddush
Sanctification, a blessing recited over wine to sanctify the Shabbat at Jewish holidays.
Laodicea
Ancient city built on the River Lycus in the Roman Province in Asia. One of the early centers of Christianity.
Megiddo
Ancient city situated in Northern Israel near Kibbutz, about 30 km south of Haifa, Israel.

Glossary Continued

Mitzvot
Refers to precepts and commandments commanded by God.

Parsha
A section of biblical text in the Masoretic text of the Tanach: (Hebrew Bible)

Seleucia
A Mesopotamian city of the Seleucid Parthian and Sasanian Empire.

Shabbat
Jewish day of rest and seventh day of rest.

Shalom
Perfect peace of God. Jewish greeting.

Tefillin
A small black leather box containing scrolls of parchment with straps of leather.

Tallit
A fringed garment traditionally worn over one's clothing by Jewish men.

Tunic
A light or heavy garment worn by men, usually with a belt or cloth fabric around the waist. They come in various colors.

Yamaka
A brimless cap, usually made of cloth worn by Jews to fulfill the customary requirements of the synagogue.

Yeshua HaMashiach
"Jesus Christ" in Hebrew.

Zion
Jerusalem

חי

Hebrew lettering for "life."

Follow the Sign

After writing the first twelve chapters of this book, I found this article and pictures of the oldest Christian church in Israel.

By Tim Butcher in Jerusalem
12:03AM GMT 07 Nov 2005

Prisoners helped discover one of Christianity's earliest churches when they took part in an archaeological dig inside one of Israel's top security jails.

A large and superbly preserved mosaic with a Greek inscription referring to the "Lord Jesus Christ" and featuring two images of a fish, an early Christian symbol, was discovered during renovation work inside the prison at Megiddo, thought to be the modern name for the biblical site of Armageddon.

The main street in Ephesus, Turkey, of the Library of Celsus, one of the Seven Wonders of the World.

Sunset on the Mediterranean on our tour of the Greek Islands.

The Wailing Wall in Jerusalem.

A view of the Caryatides at Athens, Greece.

A view of the West Bank and the Jordan Valley from the Golan Heights in Israel.

Wading in the Jordan River in Israel.

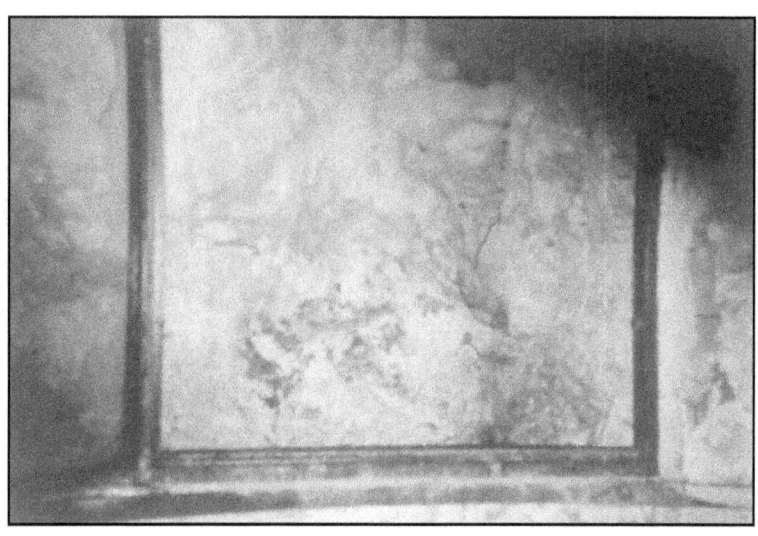

A view of a vault line in the Mount of Olives in Jerusalem.

The Domitian Temple in Ephesus, Turkey.

In front of the Torah in Abukav Synagogue,
the oldest operating synagogue in Israel today.

After speaking with a Rabbi about my Jewish heritage,
I was invited to Shabbat with the congregation.

The temple of Hephaistos in Athens, Greece.

View of Mesada, Israel.

Standing in front of the Library Celsus in Ephesus.

About the Author

Gralin W. Buratt

Gralin W. Buratt is a Messianic Jew dedicated to bringing the knowledge of Yeshua to unbelievers, Jews, and Christians. He continues to present the "Torah to Calvary" teaching.

For many years following his pastoral work, G.W. has been doing missionary work, with extensive work in Mexico, Pakistan, and India. He also teaches and speaks in all church denominations.

www.ingramcontent.com/pod-product-compliance
Lightning Source LLC
LaVergne TN
LVHW051842080426
835512LV00018B/3033